Business Guide To Avoiding Environmental Liability

Thomas M. Downs

Swidler & Berlin, Chartered

 Government Institutes, Inc.

Government Institutes, Inc., Rockville, Maryland 20850

ISBN : 0-86587-349-6

Library of Congress Catalog Card Number: 93-80176

Printed in the United States of America

BUSINESS GUIDE TO AVOIDING ENVIRONMENTAL LIABILITY

TABLE OF CONTENTS
Overview

	Page
PREFACE	x
ABOUT THE AUTHOR	xii
ACKNOWLEDGEMENTS	xii
CHAPTER 1 GROWING FEDERAL AND STATE PROSECUTIONS OF ENVIRONMENTAL CRIMES	1
CHAPTER 2: RECOGNIZING WHAT CONSTITUTES AN ENVIRONMENTAL CRIME	11
CHAPTER 3: UNDERSTANDING THE ENVIRONMENTAL STATUTORY FRAMEWORK	26
CHAPTER 4: ASSESSING THE COSTS AND RISKS OF USING ENVIRONMENTAL AUDITS TO IDENTIFY AND CORRECT VIOLATIONS	46
CHAPTER 5: PROTECTING YOURSELF WHEN WORKING WITH OUTSIDE CONTRACTORS: CONTRACT TIPS AND PITFALLS	58
CHAPTER 6: HOW REGULATORS PICK THEIR TARGETS FOR ENVIRONMENTAL CRIMINAL PROSECUTION	71
CHAPTER 7: RESPONDING APPROPRIATELY TO CRIMINAL INVESTIGATIONS	83
CHAPTER 8: THE FEDERAL SENTENCING GUIDELINES AND ENVIRONMENTAL CRIME PENALTIES	91
APPENDICES	99

BUSINESS GUIDE TO AVOIDING
ENVIRONMENTAL LIABILITY

TABLE OF CONTENTS

                                                                    Page

PREFACE x

ABOUT THE AUTHOR xii

ACKNOWLEDGEMENTS xii

CHAPTER 1. GROWING FEDERAL AND STATE PROSECUTIONS
            OF ENVIRONMENTAL CRIMES 1

1.1   ZEALOUS FEDERAL ENFORCEMENT 1

1.2   ENVIRONMENTAL CRIMINAL PROSECUTIONS
      OF CORPORATE AMERICA 3

1.3   STATE AND LOCAL PROSECUTION 6

1.4   JOINT FEDERAL-STATE ENFORCEMENT 10

CHAPTER 2. RECOGNIZING WHAT CONSTITUTES AN
            ENVIRONMENTAL CRIME 11

2.1   REGULATORY CRIMES 11

2.2   THE RESPONSIBLE CORPORATE OFFICER DOCTRINE 17

2.3   THE RESPONSIBLE CORPORATE OFFICER DOCTRINE IN
      FEDERAL STATUTES 21

2.4   THE RESPONSIBLE CORPORATE OFFICER DOCTRINE IN
      STATE STATUTES 23

2.5   COLLECTIVE KNOWLEDGE DOCTRINE 25

<u>Page</u>

CHAPTER 3. UNDERSTANDING THE ENVIRONMENTAL
STATUTORY FRAMEWORK 26

3.1 FEDERAL ENVIRONMENTAL STATUTES 26

    3.1.1 The Clean Air Act 27

        3.1.1.A In General 27

        3.1.1.B Emission Restrictions 28

        3.1.1.C False Statements 28

        3.1.1.D Failure to Pay Fees 29

        3.1.1.E Negligent Endangerment 29

        3.1.1.F Knowing Endangerment 30

        3.1.1.G Increased Prosecutions Against
Corporations and Corporate Officers
and Employees Under The Clean Air Act 31

    3.1.2 The Clean Water Act 32

        3.1.2.A Original Clean Water Act Criminal Provisions . 32

        3.1.2.B Water Quality Act of 1987 33

    3.1.3 THE RESOURCE CONSERVATION AND RECOVERY ACT
("RCRA") 36

        3.1.3.A Criminal Provisions 36

        3.1.3.B "Knowing Endangerment" 37

Page

3.1.4   REPORTING VIOLATIONS UNDER CERCLA AND
        EPCRA 38

3.1.5   REGULATION OF CHEMICALS AND OTHER FEDERAL
        STATUTES 39

        3.1.5.A   The Federal Insecticide Fungicide
                   and Rodenticide Act ("FIFRA") 39

        3.1.5.B   The Toxic Substances Control Act ("TSCA") ... 40

        3.1.5.C   The Occupational Safety and Health Act
                   ("OSHA"): Criminal Penalty
                   Reform 41

        3.1.5.D   Other Federal Statutes and
                   Continuing Attention to Environ-
                   mental Crimes in Federal Statutes 42

3.2   GENERAL CRIMINAL STATUTES 42

3.3   THE CRIMINAL FINES IMPROVEMENTS ACT OF 1987 44

CHAPTER 4: ASSESSING THE COSTS AND RISKS OF USING
            ENVIRONMENTAL AUDITS TO IDENTIFY AND
            CORRECT VIOLATIONS 46

4.1   GOVERNMENT ENCOURAGEMENT OF AUDITS 46

4.2   COSTS AND RISKS OF ENVIRONMENTAL AUDITS 51

4.3   THE COMPLIANCE DIAGNOSTIC 51

4.4   PROTECTING CONFIDENTIALITY OF AUDIT INFORMATION . 56

CHAPTER 5: PROTECTING YOURSELF WHEN WORKING WITH
            OUTSIDE CONTRACTORS: CONTRACT TIPS AND
            PITFALLS 58

5.1   INTRODUCTION 58

Page

5.2   THE ROLE OF THE ENVIRONMENTAL CONTRACTOR 58

5.3   CONTRACTS WITH ENVIRONMENTAL CONTRACTORS AND
       CONSULTANTS 59

       5.3.A   General Advice 59

       5.3.B   Specific Contract Issues 61

                5.3.B.1   Standard of Care 61

                5.3.B.2   Exclusive Use Provision 62

                5.3.B.3   Independent Contractor Status 62

                5.3.B.4   Approval of Subcontractors 63

                5.3.B.5   Indemnification 63

                5.3.B.6   Limitations of Liability 65

                5.3.B.7   Major Changes and Delays 65

                5.3.B.8   Condition of the Site 66

                5.3.B.9   Disposal of Wastes 67

                5.3.B.10   Insurance 67

                5.3.B.11   Key Personnel 68

                5.3.B.12   Laboratories 68

                5.3.B.13   Retention and Confidentiality of Records 69

                5.3.B.14   Warranty of Non-Disbarment 70

  Page

5.4   CONCLUSION 70

CHAPTER 6: HOW REGULATORS PICK THEIR TARGETS FOR
            ENVIRONMENTAL CRIMINAL PROSECUTION 71

6.1   INTRODUCTION 71

6.2   DEPARTMENT OF JUSTICE GUIDANCE 72

       6.2.1   Voluntary Disclosure 73

       6.2.2   Cooperation 74

       6.2.3   Preventive Measures and Compliance
                Programs 74

       6.2.4   Pervasiveness of Noncompliance 76

       6.2.5   Internal Disciplinary Action 76

       6.2.6   Subsequent Compliance Efforts 77

6.3   OTHER FACTORS RELEVANT TO THE EXERCISE OF
       PROSECUTORIAL DISCRETION 77

       6.3.1   Criminal Actions Against Companies 77

       6.3.2   Criminal Actions Against Individuals 79

6.4   STEPS TO REDUCE THE LIKELIHOOD OF BEING A
       TARGET OF A CRIMINAL ENFORCEMENT ACTION 80

CHAPTER 7: RESPONDING APPROPRIATELY TO CRIMINAL
            INVESTIGATIONS 83

7.1   GOVERNMENT USE OF SEARCH WARRANTS 83

Page

7.2   LIMITS ON SEARCH WARRANTS 84

7.3   RECEIPT OF THE WARRANT/MONITORING THE
        INVESTIGATION 85

CHAPTER 8:   THE FEDERAL SENTENCING GUIDELINES AND
                      ENVIRONMENTAL CRIME PENALTIES 91

8.1   SENTENCING GUIDELINES FOR INDIVIDUALS 91

8.2   SENTENCING GUIDELINES FOR ORGANIZATIONS 94

        8.2.1   Fines 95

        8.2.2   Probation and Other Non-Monetary Penalties 97

APPENDICES 99

APPENDIX A: U.S. Justice Department Procedures Between
                          U.S. Attorneys' Offices and DOJ Headquarters
                          Recent Amendments to Chapter 11 of Title 5
                          of the United States Attorneys' Manual
                          (Jan. 13, 1993) 101

APPENDIX B: New Jersey Voluntary Environmental
                          Audit/Compliance Guidelines 114

APPENDIX C: U.S. Department of Justice, Factors in
                          Decisions on Criminal Prosecutions for
                          Environmental Violations in the Context
                          of Significant Voluntary Compliance or
                          Disclosure Efforts by the Violator
                          (July 1, 1991) 121

APPENDIX D: Working Draft Recommendations by the
                          Advisory Working Group on Environmental
                          Sanctions to the United States Sentencing
                          Commission 132

PREFACE

> I want to remember the splendid skies of the city I love and the Everglades and the coral reefs that I've explored all my life, and I want to see that the laws of this country are enforced in every way possible to protect the environment.[*]
>
> -- Janet Reno, U.S. Attorney General

> I have come to believe that we must take bold and unequivocal action: we must make the rescue of the environment the central organizing principle for civilization . . . [this] means embarking on an all-out effort to use every policy and program, every law and institution, every treaty and alliance, every tactic and strategy, every plan and course of action -- to use, in short, every means to halt the destruction of the environment and to preserve and nurture our ecological system.[**]
>
> -- Vice President Albert Gore

---

[*]   Opening Statement of Janet Reno before the Senate Judiciary Committee, March 9, 1993.

[**]   Senator Albert Gore, *Earth in the Balance; Ecology and the Human Spirit*, 269, 274 (1992).

As environmental enforcement activities accelerate it is critical for organizations to have in place environmental policies and programs which will lead to the detection and prevention of violations. Now more than ever, businesses must be on guard against potential environmental violations. Businesses must begin to take preventive and precautionary measures to reduce the likelihood of environmental violations. This will require the adoption and implementation of corporate policies and programs that promote and achieve environmental compliance. Should violations occur, organizations must know how to reduce the likelihood of criminal prosecution and to prevent information gathered in connection with compliance programs from being used against them by prosecutors.

This handbook is designed to inform businesses of the key issues in the enforcement of environmental laws. The handbook also provides specific guidance to help businesses develop environmental compliance programs and procedures to respond to investigations.

The handbook is organized into eight chapters. Chapter 1 provides an overview of trends in environmental enforcement and legislation. This chapter identifies the goals of the Environmental Protection Agency, the Department of Justice, and state enforcement agencies in environmental cases. The chapter also describes the historic growth in environmental crimes prosecutions and penalties. Chapter 2 describes the general components of environmental crimes. Chapter 3 describes the major Federal environmental statutes. Chapter 4 discusses the value of environmental audits. This chapter provides a suggested approach to environmental audits. Chapter 4 also includes specific suggestions for protecting the confidentiality of audit information. Chapter 5 identifies ways businesses can protect themselves from environmental liability when working with outside contractors. Chapter 6 describes how prosecutors pick their targets. Chapter 7 provides specific recommendations for responding to a criminal investigation. Chapter 8 describes the Federal Sentencing Guidelines, including the draft Federal Sentencing Guidelines for sentencing organizations convicted of Federal environmental crimes.

ABOUT THE AUTHOR

Thomas M. Downs has practiced environmental law since 1968. He has served as Assistant Attorney General of Maryland, Deputy Director of the Maryland Department of Water Resources and Secretary of the Maryland Council on the Environment.

Since entering private practice in 1976, Mr. Downs has represented clients in administrative, civil and criminal environmental litigation throughout the country. He has extensive trial and appellate experience.

Mr. Downs' publications include <u>Recent Developments in Environmental Crime</u> (1991), <u>Compliance Planning and Auditing in Light of the Corporate Sentencing Guidelines</u> (1992), <u>Responding to Search Warrants and Grand Jury Subpoenas in Environmental Cases</u> (1993) and an upcoming book entitled, <u>Business Guide to Avoiding Environmental Liability</u>.

Mr. Downs is Vice Chair of the American Bar Association's Committee on Environmental Crime and Enforcement.

ACKNOWLEDGEMENTS

Shelley L. Spencer, Lynn M. Gallagher and Arjun Goswami generously contributed their time and expertise to the production of this guide.

CHAPTER 1
GROWING FEDERAL AND STATE PROSECUTIONS
OF ENVIRONMENTAL CRIMES

1.1   ZEALOUS FEDERAL ENFORCEMENT

The U.S. Environmental Protection Agency ("EPA") has primary responsibility for investigating violations of and enforcing Federal environmental laws. Over the past seven years, EPA referrals of possible criminal violations of environmental laws to the U.S. Department of Justice have increased by 300%, prosecutions have increased by 1000%, and convictions by 700%.

The number of criminal prosecutions of environmental crimes is unprecedented. In March of 1993, the Chief of the U.S. Department Justice's Environmental Crimes Section ("ECS") told a committee of the American Bar Association that the number of environmental crime indictments had increased by 50% and the number of trials by 100% in the first six months of fiscal 1993.[1] During the fiscal years 1988-1992, the U.S. Department of Justice obtained 551 indictments for environmental crimes. These indictments culminated in 94% of all the criminal penalties ever imposed under Federal environmental laws and 69% of the actual jail time imposed in the history of U.S. criminal environmental

---

[1]   Federal environmental crimes cases may be prosecuted by members of the ECS, United States Attorneys, or jointly. The Department of Justice's procedures for prosecuting environmental crimes are set forth in Appendix A.

enforcement.[2/] A record 191 criminal indictments were issued in 1992. Federal criminal prosecutions of environmental crimes in 1992 yielded a record $163 million in penalties and 34 years of imprisonment. Indictments of corporate officers were up from 71 in the previous year to 103 in 1992. Environmental crime prosecutions result in a windfall for the Federal government. Currently, for every one dollar spent for prosecution, $24 is returned to the government by way of fines and penalties.

Increasing political pressure is likely to accelerate the aggressive prosecution of environmental crimes. Congress has begun to question decisions by Federal prosecutors not to prosecute organizations or their officers for environmental crimes. For example, representatives of the U.S. Department of Justice's ECS have been called before Congressional committees to explain plea negotiations and plea bargains.

In a report submitted to Congressman Charles E. Schumer, Chairman of the U.S. House of Representatives Judiciary Committee's Subcommittee on Crime and Criminal Justice, the Environmental Crimes Project of the George Washington University performed an analysis of several environmental crimes cases that had been referred to the ECS. The report recommended more aggressive prosecution

---

[2/]   Department of Justice, *Department of Justice Announces Record $2 Billion Year for Environmental Enforcement* (Oct. 29, 1992).

of environmental crimes.[3/]   The ongoing debate over the prosecution of environmental crimes will likely result in a significant increase in the number of environmental criminal prosecutions at the Federal and state levels.

1.2   ENVIRONMENTAL CRIMINAL PROSECUTIONS OF CORPORATE AMERICA

One of the dangers companies and executives face with regard to environmental crime may result from their failure to realize the extent to which corporate America and corporate officials are the targets of enforcement action. There are several prevailing myths. First, there is the myth that only so-called "midnight dumpers" are prosecuted. Second, there is a myth that only people with dirty hands are likely to be prosecuted and that strict instructions to employees to obey environmental laws will protect the corporation and the corporate hierarchy. A careful examination of recent environmental prosecutions dispels these myths.

Targets of environmental crimes prosecutions are not limited to "midnight dumpers" but often include corporate officers and managers in well-known corporations. A survey of criminal defendants in environmental cases shows a

---

[3/]   Environmental Crimes Project, National Law Center, George Washington University, *Preliminary Report on Criminal Environmental Prosecution by the United States Department of Justice* (Oct. 19, 1992) at 5.

number of Fortune 500 and other prominent companies such as Ciba-Geigy, Exxon, Pennwalt and Union Carbide. Corporations large and small face the scrutiny of environmental prosecutors. For example, in 1992, Bristol-Myers Squibb Co. was fined $3.5 million for violations of the Clean Water Act. Under its plea agreement, Bristol-Myers will build a wastewater treatment facility at an estimated cost of $10-30 million. These penalties came after the company invested $35 million to upgrade its environmental systems.[4] Exxon received the largest environmental fine in history, $1.15 billion, as a result of the Exxon Valdez spill.[5]

The effects of tough environmental prosecution on individuals and on small companies can be particularly devastating. In 1987, Welco Plating Company pleaded guilty to violations of hazardous waste laws and paid a $1.3 million fine which drove it out of business. The owner of the company was fined $200,000 and sentenced to 18 months in prison.[6] Indeed, it seems jail time has been imposed on the owners and operators of small to mid-sized companies more often than on

---

[4]   *United States v. Bristol-Myers Squibb Co.*, No. 92-CR-123 (N.D.N.Y., Apr. 24, 1992), *cited in* "Bristol-Myers to Pay Fine, Build Treatment Plant to Settle Charges of Water Pollution Violations," 23 Environment Reporter (BNA) 20 (May 1, 1992).

[5]   *U.S. v. Exxon Corp.*, Nos. A-91-082-CV and A-90-0152-CR (D. Alaska); *Alaska v. Exxon Corp.*, No. A-91-083-CV (D. Alaska) (settlement approved Oct. 8, 1991).

[6]   *See* Frank E. Allen, "Few Big Firms Get Jail Time for Polluting," Wall St. J., Dec. 9, 1991, at B1.

officers and directors of large corporations.[7]

In November 1990, Justice Department officials from the Department's Environment and Natural Resources Division stated that more corporate officials were prosecuted in the fiscal year 1990 for environmental crimes than at any time in the past. Former Attorney General Richard Thornburgh noted that 78% of the targets in fiscal 1990 were corporations and their top officers and that "more than half of the individuals convicted for environmental crimes [in 1990] were given prison sentences and 84% of these [were] actually serving real jail time."[8] Richard B. Stewart, then Assistant Attorney General of the Environment and Natural Resources Division, noted that "most prosecutions [were] against corporations and their top officers [averaging] fine[s] over $181,000. In 1990, 55% of the individuals indicted [were] given jail time with the average time served of 1.8 years."[9] Convictions of corporate officials are increasing. In March of 1993, a Texas jury convicted the former chief executive of a ceramics firm which employed more than

---

[7]   An independent study by a Vanderbilt Business School Professor indicated that 25% of those jailed for environmental crimes were from small companies compared to 9% from large businesses. *See* Karen Heller, "Clamping Down on Environmental Crime; Enforcement Toughens, Penalties Rise," Chemical Week, Apr. 1, 1992, at 22.

[8]   *See* "Prosecution of Corporate Officials Reaches Record," BNA's National Environment Watch, Vol. 1, No. 33 at 1 (Nov. 26, 1990).

[9]   R.B. Stewart, Criminal Environmental Enforcement, (ALI-ABA, April 11-12, 1991) at 3.

5,000 workers. He was convicted of 16 violations of the Resource Conservation and Recovery Act and faces up to 35 years in prison and $4.5 million in fines. The conviction involved transportation and disposal of lead contaminated process byproducts. In 1986, Neils Hoyvald, President of Beech-Nut Nutrition Corp. was convicted of environmental crimes.[10/] Although the guilty verdict was overturned on appeal, Hoyvald later accepted a plea bargain and entered a guilty plea.

1.3 STATE AND LOCAL PROSECUTION

The vigorous nature of Federal criminal enforcement should not overshadow the importance and seriousness of state and local prosecutions. Despite a lack of reliable data concerning state enforcement actions, it is widely believed that the vast majority of environmental enforcement actions are on the state level. EPA has begun a pilot program to gather state enforcement data and plans to incorporate that data into its 1994 Enforcement Report. Although various states have taken different approaches to environmental crimes prosecutions, most states are intensifying their efforts.

New Jersey, for example, has made "a significant commitment of both manpower and resources to the enforcement of environmental laws and

---

[10/]   *United States v. Beech-Nut Nutrition Corp.*, 677 F. Supp. 117 (E.D.N.Y. 1987).

regulations."[11]   In New Jersey, various departments including the Attorney General's office, the Environmental Protection and Energy Department ("EPED) and the Board of Public Utilities have environmental enforcement units. On January 24, 1990, the Governor of New Jersey created the Office of the State Environmental Prosecutor ("OSEP") and the State Environmental Prosecutor ("SEP") in order to centralize and coordinate the state's environmental crime efforts.

This added increased vigor to New Jersey's prosecutorial efforts, the results of which were evident in the resolution of a case involving Exxon and an inter-refinery pipeline rupture. Following a twelve month criminal investigation by EPED and the Division of Criminal Justice, Exxon entered a guilty plea to criminal negligence in violation of the Federal Clean Water Act. Civil and criminal charges led to Exxon's payment of $15 million to New York, New Jersey and the U.S. Government. This payment was in addition to $44 million Exxon had paid previously.

Consistent with its leading position in state enforcement of environmental laws, the New Jersey OSEP has published Voluntary Environmental Audit and

---

[11]   *See* Steven J. Madonna, "New Jersey's Office of Environmental Prosecutor," National Environmental Enforcement Journal, Vol. 6, No. 7 at 3, August 1991.

Compliance Guidelines.[12] These guidelines encourage New Jersey businesses to adopt voluntary environmental compliance and audit programs. Under the guidelines, prosecutors can consider implementation and operation of such programs as mitigating factors in exercising their criminal enforcement discretion. New Jersey also has an innovative whistle blower statute that encourages citizen involvement in environmental prosecutions.

Similarly, in Minnesota, the Attorney General and the Pollution Control Agency Commissioner formed the Minnesota Environmental Crimes Team (ECT).[13] The case of *Minnesota v. Marvin Lumber & Cedar Co. d/b/a Marvin Windows* provides an illustration of the ECT's success.[14] Following an investigation by ECT, the defendant entered a guilty plea to illegal storage of hazardous waste and agreed to pay a $2 million fine.

There also is a movement toward state criminal prosecution of corporate executives for manslaughter and homicide in cases where improper use of

---

[12] Robert J. Del Tufo and Steven J. Madonna, *New Jersey Voluntary Environmental Audit/Compliance Guidelines* (May 15, 1992). The guidelines are set forth in Appendix B.

[13] *See* Alan R. Mitchell, "The Minnesota Environmental Crimes Team," National Environmental Enforcement Journal, Vol. 6, No. 6 at 3, July 1991.

[14] No. K4-90-715 (D.Ct. Rouseau County, Nov. 28, 1990).

hazardous or toxic substances results in a death.[15]

● On March 9, 1993 an Arizona Grand Jury indicted the former owner of a Tucson, Arizona company on criminal charges of extreme indifference for human life in the improper storage of hazardous wastes.[16] The indictment stems from an April 1992 investigation which revealed a plastic container of hydrochloric acid held together by make-shift metal banding was stored within 20 feet of a cyanide plating line. The indictment charges the defendant with storing hazardous waste for more than 90 days without a permit; storing waste in containers without proper marking; and close storage of incompatible wastes.

● On August 28, 1991, a second degree manslaughter charge was brought against a New York businessman who prosecutors contended paid for the illegal dumping of toxic wastes that killed a man.[17]

● In Ohio, a company was charged with involuntary manslaughter in the death of an employee killed in an explosion and fire.[18] The State alleged that the company's practices for handling safety, training and hazardous waste were insufficient and that proper management could have prevented the explosion and fire. The corporation entered a plea of no contest to the involuntary manslaughter charge and to the charge of illegal transportation of hazardous waste and polluting the waters. The company's president entered a plea of no contest to a misdemeanor count of criminal endangerment.

---

[15] *See New York v. Pymm*, 563 N.E.2d 1 (N.Y. 1990), *cert. den.*, 111 S. Ct. 958 (1991); *Michigan v. Hegedus*, 443 N.W.2d 127 (Mich. 1989); *Illinois v. Chicago Magnet Wire Corp.*, 534 N.E.2d 962, (Ill.), *cert. den.*, 110 S. Ct. 52 (1989).

[16] *Arizona v. Swain*, #CR40820, (Super. Ct. Pima County).

[17] *See* "Manslaughter Charged in Waste Dumping case," *The Washington Post*, August 29, 1991, at A6.

[18] *Ohio v. Wiley Organics, Inc., d/b/a Organic Technologies*, No. 92-CR-359 (C.P. Licking County, Oct. 5, 1992).

1.4   JOINT FEDERAL-STATE ENFORCEMENT

Hoping to draw on the efforts of state prosecutors, EPA is making an effort to combine Federal and state actions. EPA has taken the position that better cooperation between state and Federal regulators will influence the degree of enforcement. EPA and state administrators have begun to explore ways to improve cooperation.[19]

---

[19]   *See* Catherine Cooney, "Tate Seeks States' Aid on Enforcement," Environment Week, Apr. 16, 1992.

CHAPTER 2

RECOGNIZING WHAT CONSTITUTES AN ENVIRONMENTAL CRIME

2.1   REGULATORY CRIMES

Most environmental crimes defendants, whether corporate or individual, are shocked upon learning how easily the government can establish criminal liability. In large measure, such ease is attributable to the erosion of the element of criminal intent in environmental crimes. Historically, criminal laws have required that the defendant have a certain state of mind or *mens rea*. Increasingly, courts are moving away from the conventional requirement of criminal intent in favor of protecting the larger "public good."

In 1943, the U.S. Supreme Court stated that:

> Such [regulatory] legislation dispenses with the conventional requirement for criminal conduct -- awareness of some wrongdoing. In the interest of the larger good it puts the burden of acting at hazard upon a person otherwise innocent but standing in responsible relation to a public danger.[20]

Legislatures may freely choose to dispense with any requirement of criminal intent and create regulatory offenses. These so-called regulatory crimes may impose strict liability and criminal liability in the absence of any clearly discernible

---

[20]   *United States v. Dotterweich*, 64 S. Ct. 134, 136 (1943).

wrongdoing, certainly without proof of any purposeful violation of the law. Businesses subject to environmental regulation and those who operate them cannot afford to ignore the risks that may result. More than ever before, scrupulous if not perfect compliance is the only safe course.

The criminal intent requirement of many environmental crimes has been eroded by the courts' interpretation of statutes that impose criminal penalties for "knowing" violations. The courts have been inconsistent in determining when violations must be "knowingly" committed and in determining what measure of proof is sufficient to establish a "knowing" violation. Several courts have addressed the concept of "knowing" violations under the Resource Conservation and Recovery Act ("RCRA"). For example, in *Johnson & Towers*,[21] two corporate employees were charged individually with violating a RCRA provision that made liable:

[a]ny person who --

(2) knowingly treats, stores, or disposes of any hazardous waste identified or listed under this subchapter either --

(A) without having obtained a permit under 6925 of this title . . . or

(B) in knowing violation of any material condition or requirement of such permit.[22]

---

[21] 741 F.2d 662 (3rd Cir. 1984), *cert. den.*, 105 S. Ct. 1171 (1985).

[22] 42 U.S.C. § 6928(d) (1982). The statute has been amended since *Johnson v. Towers* was decided. The same substantive requirement remains in effect despite the amendment.

On appeal the appellate court interpreted the meaning of "knowingly" in the statute to extend to knowledge that the company did not have the required permit. The court held that the knowledge of the absence of a permit was an element of the crime, to be proved beyond a reasonable doubt like every other element. The opinion rejected a strict liability construction of the RCRA criminal provision. But the court proceeded from this conclusion to two further conclusions about the statute. First, the court held that "the government need prove only knowledge of the actions taken and not of the statute forbidding them."[23/] Second, the court said that the jury could infer knowledge, including that of the permit requirement, by those individuals who hold "the requisite responsible positions with the corporate defendant."[24/] While the court required that the defendants have a certain *mens rea*, it diluted the requirement by permitting the government to prove knowledge by inference.

Other courts have adhered to the criminal intent requirement by requiring the government to prove that the crime was committed "knowingly." For example, in *United States v. Hayes International Corp.*,[25/] the appellate court held in a RCRA prosecution under § 6298(d)(1) that jurors, drawing inferences from all of the

---

[23/]   741 F.2d at 669.

[24/]   *Id.* at 670.

[25/]   786 F.2d 1499 (11th Cir. 1986).

circumstances, including the existence of the regulatory scheme, must find that a defendant knew what the waste was and that the disposal site had no permit.

In *United States v. MacDonald & Watson Waste Oil Co.,*[26] another appellate court addressed the intent that must be proved in a RCRA prosecution under § 6928(d)(1). The court approved a trial court's instruction that the prosecution must prove that the defendant knew that the facility lacked a proper permit, or "willfully failed to determine" whether it had the necessary permit. The court said that there was "much to be said" for requiring proof of such knowledge.[27] Similarly, in *United States v. Baytank (Houston), Inc.,*[28] the court concluded in a prosecution under § 6928(d)(2)(A) that Congress's use of the term "knowingly" "means no more than that the defendant knows factually what he is doing -- storing, what is being stored, and that what is being stored factually has the potential for harm to others or the environment, and that he has no permit -- and it is not required that he know that there is a regulation which says what he is storing is hazardous under the RCRA."[29]

---

[26] 933 F.2d 35 (1st Cir. 1991).

[27] *Id.* at 47-48.

[28] 934 F.2d 599 (5th Cir. 1991).

[29] *Id.* at 613.

In a 1989 decision in *United States v. Hoflin*,[30] an appellate court held that "knowledge of the absence of a permit is not an element of the offense defined by 42 U.S.C. § 6928(d)(2)(A)."[31] The court also dispensed with a requirement of proof that the defendant knew that a permit was required. The court required only "that the defendant knew the material being disposed of was hazardous."[32] In *United States v. Dean*,[33] a manager was convicted of storing and disposing of hazardous wastes without a permit in violation of 42 U.S.C. § 6928(d)(2)(A). The court held that knowledge of a permit requirement was not required in order to convict the defendant. In *United States v. Goldsmith*,[34] the court held that the government need not prove that a defendant knew a waste was a hazardous waste. It needed to prove only that the defendant knew the general hazardous character of the chemical to sustain a conviction.

The judicial and legislative erosion of criminal intent as an element of environmental crime leads to several conclusions that should be evaluated by

---

[30]   880 F.2d 1033 (9th Cir. 1989), *cert. den.*, 110 S. Ct. 1143 (1990).

[31]   *Id.* at 1039.

[32]   *Id.*

[33]   969 F.2d 187 (6th Cir. 1992), *cert. den.*, 113 S. Ct. 1852 (1993).

[34]   978 F.2d 643 (11th Cir. 1992).

business in the context of their day-to-day operations:

> ● corporate managers, owners and directors are at risk of criminal prosecution, despite a lack of intent to violate the law.

> ● compliance -- as nearly complete as possible -- is more important than ever. Ignorance will not provide a reliable defense in a criminal prosecution for environmental violations. Deliberate ignorance or "willful blindness" will provide no defense, even when a criminal statute requires proof of the defendant's knowledge.

> ● Steps can be taken to avoid prosecution. An environmental audit or diagnostic is often a necessary first step.

If a criminal prosecution is threatened, or if prosecution begins before a preventive program is implemented, the intent elements of the statutes can be utilized as a defense and to negotiate with the prosecution. Despite deep and broad public concern over the environment, juries resist convicting individuals unfairly. When a jury is properly instructed, and when it hears sufficiently compelling evidence of a defendant's lack of wrongful intent or knowledge, an acquittal can be won.

The absence of criminal intention should be pushed at all stages: in dealings with the government to stave off criminal prosecution, in efforts to avoid indictment, in pre-trial motions and instruction requests, before the jury at trial and if necessary on appeal. All opportunities that the relevant statute may provide should be exploited, so that a lack of criminal intent can be urged as the basis for a successful defense.

2.2   THE RESPONSIBLE CORPORATE OFFICER DOCTRINE

The responsible corporate officer (RCO) is a doctrine used by environmental prosecutors to hold corporate officers responsible for environmental crimes.[35/] The RCO doctrine extends the criminal liability of corporate officers and managers beyond the acts actually performed by the corporate officers or managers. Furthermore, under the RCO doctrine, a corporate officer is exposed to individual criminal liability even if the officer's acts were at the corporation's direction. In its most expansive form, the RCO doctrine can result in felony convictions of corporate officers if the officers had a "reasonable relationship" to the violation. Convictions have been upheld under this doctrine even if the corporate officers had no knowledge of the problem and acted reasonably in attempting to keep the corporation in compliance with the law. The RCO doctrine is gaining acceptance in the courts and being incorporated into environmental statutes.

The expansive nature of the RCO doctrine is best illustrated by selected individual cases in which it has been applied. The primary case that established the

---

[35/]   The RCO doctrine has been applied in civil enforcement actions as well as criminal prosecutions. In civil cases, courts have found corporate officers personally liable because they influence corporate policy and practices.

theory of imposing criminal liability on responsible corporate officers is the U.S. Supreme Court's decision in *United States v. Park.*[36/] Park was president and chief executive officer of Acme Markets, Inc., a national food chain. Rodents had infested an Acme warehouse and Park was warned of the problem. He conferred with the corporation's vice president for legal affairs and learned that the responsible division vice president "'was investigating the situation immediately and would be preparing a summary of the corrective action to reply to the [FDA's warning] letter.'"[37/] At trial, Park testified that his position made him ultimately responsible for "'any result which occurs in our company,'" although he did not "'believe there was anything [he] could have done more constructively than what [he] found was being done,'" to combat the rats in Acme's warehouse.[38/]

The Supreme Court upheld Park's conviction. The Court found the government's case sufficient "to warrant a finding . . . that the defendant had, by reason of his position in the corporation, responsibility and authority either to prevent in the first instance, or promptly to correct, the violation complained of, and that he failed to do so."[39/]

[36/]   25 S. Ct. 1903 (1975).

[37/]   *Id.* at 1907.

[38/]   *Id.* at 1907-08.

[39/]   *Id.* at 1912.

The Supreme Court's decision establishes a far-reaching principle of criminal liability for corporate officers or employees who stand in a *responsible relationship* to activities of the corporation that violate Federal criminal laws. As a rule of liability within a corporate structure, this holding offers few refuges for corporate officers and managers from the risk of criminal prosecution. Corporate officers and managers can be held liable for everything within their general domain whether or not they are aware of the problem.

Although originally applied in the context of food regulation, the RCO doctrine has been used in environmental law to prosecute corporate officers and managers who hold responsible positions within a corporation. For example, in *Johnson & Towers*, two employees who managed and directed a corporation's treatment, storage, and disposal of hazardous wastes and pollutants were charged individually with violating RCRA. The district court held that the statute's criminal provisions only applied to "owners and operators," who were obligated to obtain a permit and dismissed these counts against the defendants. On appeal, the decision was reversed and the employees were found subject to criminal prosecution under RCRA if they knew or should have known that the company had failed to comply with the permit requirements of RCRA.

The court held that knowledge of the absence of a permit was an element of the crime, that had to be proven like every other element. However, the court permitted the jury to infer knowledge, including knowledge of the permit requirement, to those individuals who hold the requisite responsible positions with the corporation. Thus, if the defendant's job responsibilities would naturally have made him aware both of the environmental permit requirements, and of the organization's compliance, then the jury might conclude that the defendant was in fact aware of the requirements and the organization's compliance. Significantly, the court did not provide that the defendant's "responsible position" in a corporation could substitute for proof of actual knowledge. The "responsible position" constitutes one element of proof of knowledge. Courts have reversed convictions under RCRA based on the trial court's error in instructing the jury that evidence of the defendant's status could substitute for proof of actual knowledge.

The continuing vitality of the RCO doctrine also is illustrated by *U.S. v. Dee*.[40] The defendants in *Dee* were civilian engineers employed by the U.S. Army. Defendant Gepp was a chemical engineer responsible for facility operations and defendants Dee and Lentz were Gepp's superiors. As department heads, Dee and Lentz were responsible for ensuring compliance with RCRA requirements. The district court found all three defendants guilty of multiple violations of RCRA for illegally storing, treating and disposing of hazardous waste.

On appeal, the defendants argued that they did not knowingly violate RCRA.

---

[40]   912 F.2d 741 (4th Cir. 1990), *cert. den.*, 111 S. Ct. 1307 (1991).

They claimed they did not know that violating RCRA was a crime and that they were unaware that the chemicals they managed were hazardous. The appellate court affirmed the convictions and held that the government need only prove that the defendants knew the chemicals were generally of a hazardous nature. Applying the reasoning of strict liability regulatory statutes, the court stated:

> [w]here . . . dangerous or deleterious devices or products or obnoxious waste materials are involved, the probability of regulation is so great that anyone who is aware that he is in possession of them or dealing with them must be presumed to be aware of the regulation.[41]

The court's decision in *Dee* supports a continuing role for the RCO doctrine in easing the government's burden to prove the element of knowledge in RCRA prosecutions.[42]

2.3 THE RESPONSIBLE CORPORATE OFFICER DOCTRINE IN FEDERAL STATUTES

In 1992, Arthur D. Little Inc. conducted a survey on environmental crime. The survey indicated that 84% of the U.S. public felt that causing environmental

---

[41] 912 F.2d at 745, quoting *U.S. v. International Minerals*, 91 S. Ct. 1697, 1701-02 (1971).

[42] *See* Barrett & Clarke, "Perspectives on the Knowledge Requirement of Section 6928(d) of RCRA after *United States v. Dee*," 59 George Washington Law Review 862, 882 (April, 1991).

damage was a serious crime, and 75% believed that executives should be held personally liable. In this climate, Congress and state legislatures have enacted laws to encourage agencies responsible for enforcement of environmental laws to treat corporate officers as personally liable, even when they were not personally at fault for the corporation's violations.[43/] At the Federal level, criminal enforcement provisions are contained in the 1990 Amendments to the Clean Air Act. The Clean Air Act includes "responsible corporate official" within its definition of "person" and imposes individual liability on "owners," "operators" and "persons." The Clean Air Act focuses on senior management personnel and corporate officers. With the exception of knowing and willful violations, the Act excludes from liability employees carrying out their normal activities under orders from their employers.

One provision of the amended Clean Air Act requires all affected "sources" and "units" to appoint a "natural person" to serve as their "designated representative" or "DR" before receiving a permit to operate. Not only must Drs certify the truth of each statement in the permit; they must also ensure on-going compliance. Omissions or false statements may lead, in the most serious cases, to criminal penalties, including fines and jail terms. EPA's preamble to the proposed rules published in the December 3, 1991 Federal Register stated:

[43/]   *See* Trilling, "Protecting Corporate Officers from Personal Liability with an Internal Environmental Compliance Program," 6 Toxics Law Reporter (BNA) 982 (Jan. 15, 1992).

> The requirement that the designated representative be
> a natural person would not result in personal liability
> . . . in the absence of criminal wrongdoing.[44]

In addition to the Clean Air Act, the Clean Water Act's criminal provisions also incorporate the RCO doctrine. The Clean Water Act defines "persons" to include individuals, corporations, partnerships or municipalities.[45] In establishing criminal penalties, the Clean Water Act provides that "any person who knowingly or negligently" commits various acts shall be guilty of a crime. The Clean Water Act specifies that the term "person" includes "any responsible corporate officer." [46]

2.4   THE RESPONSIBLE CORPORATE OFFICER DOCTRINE IN STATE STATUTES

The RCO doctrine is being incorporated into state environmental statutes by expanding the definition of person to include "responsible corporate officers." At least nine states and the District of Columbia have enacted statutory provisions that explicitly make "responsible corporate officers" liable for certain criminal violations of environmental laws. In the states, the doctrine has been used most consistently to extend criminal liability in the area of water resources and wetlands

---

[44]   56 Fed. Reg. 63002, 63010 (Dec. 3, 1991).

[45]   33 U.S.C. § 1362(5).

[46]   33 U.S.C. § 1319(c)(6).

protection. Nine of the statutes' criminal provisions involve the protection of water resources and wetlands. The RCO doctrine has also been incorporated into state statutes that address spills of hazardous substances, compliance with hazardous waste regulations and air pollution, as shown on the following chart.

STATE	STATUTE
Alabama	Water Pollution Control Act
Connecticut	Wetlands Regulations
District of Columbia	Water Pollution Control Act
Hawaii	Water Pollution Penalties Code
Indiana	Indiana Environmental Management Act
Minnesota	Minnesota Criminal Statute
Montana	Montana Agricultural Chemical Ground Water Protection Act
New York	New York Environmental Conservation Statute
South Carolina	South Carolina Pollution Control Act
Wisconsin	Wisconsin Pollution Discharge Elimination Statute

State courts have taken an inconsistent approach to incorporation of the RCO doctrine when a state statute does not dictate its application. Some states have refused to impose criminal liability on those in managerial positions without any direct evidence of the individual's involvement in the "wrong." Other state courts have been willing to impose liability on corporate officers based on their position with the company.

2.5   COLLECTIVE KNOWLEDGE DOCTRINE

Corporations have been held responsible for the collective knowledge of all their individual agents under a "collective knowledge" theory. The collective knowledge theory is based on the premise that modern corporations "compartmentalize knowledge, subdividing the elements of specific duties and operations into smaller components."[47] Accordingly, courts determine the corporation's state of mind in regulatory offenses by considering collectively the aggregate knowledge of the corporation. The collective but separate knowledge of individual employees can expose individuals and corporations to expansive liability and prosecution for environmental crimes.

---

[47]   *United States v. Bank of New England, N.A.*, 821 F.2d 844 856 (1st Cir.), *cert. den.*, 108 S. Ct. 328 (1987).

CHAPTER 3

UNDERSTANDING THE ENVIRONMENTAL STATUTORY FRAMEWORK

There are two categories of statutory offenses for Federal prosecution of environmental wrongs: (1) general environmental statutes that include criminal provisions; and (2) criminal law provisions that are not specific to environmental crimes but have been used to address environmental harms. These more general statutes criminalize conduct such as false statements, mail fraud, wire fraud, conspiracy, aiding and abetting and obstruction of justice. While the U.S. Department of Justice's focus continues to be on Clean Water Act and RCRA violations, several cases have been brought successfully under the Clean Air Act, the Migratory Bird Treaty Act, and under the more general statutes not originally designed to address environmental issues.

3.1   FEDERAL ENVIRONMENTAL STATUTES

The number of Federal statutes governing environmental matters has increased significantly in the past decade. This chapter provides an overview of the major Federal environmental statutes as they relate to criminal enforcement. This chapter is not a comprehensive explanation of the laws' requirements. In some instances violations of these statutes may be quite technical in nature. Criminal prosecutions, however, frequently involve technical violations relating to reporting, recordkeeping, sampling procedures, laboratory procedures, monitoring methods and systems, labeling, retention time, and the handling of wastes.

3.1.1 THE CLEAN AIR ACT

The Clean Air Act, as amended in 1990, represents Congress's latest effort in environmental crimes legislation.

3.1.1.A   In General

The Clean Air Act imposes criminal liability on "any person" who knowingly violates almost any of the statute's prohibitions or requirements. The term "person" encompasses individuals, corporations, partnerships, and associations, as well as state and Federal entities. Section 113(c)(6) adds "any responsible corporate officer" to that definition.

The 1990 amendments to the Clean Air Act broadened the scope of the provisions which can yield criminal penalties and increased the penalties. With two exceptions,[48] all of the previous Clean Air Act violations have been increased from misdemeanors to felonies, with corresponding increases in the maximum fines

---

[48] Violations under Sections 113(c)(3) and (4) respectively for failure to pay fees pursuant to the Act and for negligent endangerment are misdemeanors.

and jail terms. Fines for all of the felony provisions of the Clean Air Act are a maximum of $250,000 for individual defendants and $500,000 for organizations. Fines for the misdemeanor provisions are generally limited to $100,000 for individuals and $200,000 for organizations, but may run as high as $250,000 ($500,000 for organizations) if a death results from the violation. Furthermore, all maximum fines and jail terms are doubled for any person with a prior conviction under the applicable paragraph.

3.1.1.B   Emission Restrictions

Section 113(c)(1) of the Clean Air Act makes it a felony to violate any requirement or prohibition of an applicable air quality implementation plan, or to violate virtually any substantive provision of the Act. A fine or a prison term of up to 5 years, or both, may be imposed for violations of Section 113(c)(1).

3.1.1.C   False Statements

Section 113(c)(2) of the Clean Air Act provides that any person who knowingly "makes any false material statement" or omission in, or fails to file or maintain, any document required under the Act, or who tampers with required monitoring equipment, is guilty of a felony and subject to a fine or a prison term of up to two years, or both.

3.1.1.D Failure to Pay Fees

A new Section 113(c)(3) of the Clean Air Act makes it a misdemeanor to fail knowingly to pay any fee owed to the United States under any section of the Act except those pertaining to moving sources. The applicable penalty is a fine or a prison term of up to one year, or both.

3.1.1.E Negligent Endangerment

Perhaps the most important provision added by the 1990 Amendments is Section 113(c)(4) concerning negligent endangerment. Under § 113(c)(4) of the Clean Air Act, any person who negligently releases any hazardous air pollutant, or any "extremely hazardous substance" listed in the EPA regulations, and thereby negligently places another person in "imminent danger of death or serious bodily injury," is subject to a fine or a prison term of up to one year, or both.

Although it is one of only two Clean Air Act criminal violations that is a misdemeanor, Section 113(c)(4) represents an extraordinary expansion of criminal liability by imposing such liability on *negligent* acts and omissions. While some limitation may be placed on its applicability through the limiting phrase "imminent danger of death or substantial bodily injury," the potential reach of this provision must be regarded as enormous. Because the Clean Air Act applies to any "person," including a responsible corporate officer, the negligence provision could result in a conviction for anyone in charge of environmental compliance.

3.1.1.F   Knowing Endangerment

Another felony provision added by the 1990 amendments is Section 113(c)(5), which provides for a fine or a prison term of up to 15 years, or both, for any person who knowingly releases any hazardous air pollutant, or any extremely hazardous substance, and knows at the time that the release places another person in imminent danger of death or serious bodily injury. An organization convicted under Section 113(c)(5) could be fined up to $1 million per violation. As with all violations, second offenses are subject to twice the maximum imprisonment and fine.

The scope of this provision is limited by the fact that it applies only to persons with actual knowledge. In determining whether a defendant who is an individual knew that the violation placed another person in imminent danger of death or serious bodily injury, the Act provides that "(i) the defendant is responsible only for actual awareness or actual belief possessed; and (ii) knowledge possessed by a person other than the defendant ... may not be attributed to the defendant."[49] However, circumstantial evidence may be used to prove a defendant's possession of actual knowledge, including evidence that the defendant avoided knowledge of relevant information.

3.1.1.G   Increased Prosecutions Against Corporations and Corporate Officers and Employees Under The Clean Air Act

Even under the pre-amendment Clean Air Act there were some prosecutions. For example, in *United States v. DAR Construction Inc.*[50], a corporation and its foreman were charged with asbestos-related violations. The foreman was sentenced to ninety days in jail and three years probation. The corporation was ordered to pay over $50,000 in fines. Similarly, in *United States v. Import Certification Laboratories, Inc.*[51], a company president and employees were convicted of filing false reports. The U.S. Department of Justice and EPA have

---

[49]   Clean Air Act, Section 113(c)(5)(B), 42 U.S.C. § 7413(c)(5)(B).

[50]   No. 88 Cr. 65 (S.D.N.Y. April 7, 1989) *cited in* 20 Environment Reporter (BNA) 21 (May 5, 1989).

[51]   No. CR-87-249 AWT (C.D. Cal.), *cited in* 18 Environment Reporter (BNA) 1993 (Jan. 8, 1988).

predicted that criminal prosecutions will increase under the 1990 amendments.[52]

3.1.2 THE CLEAN WATER ACT

3.1.2.A Original Clean Water Act Criminal Provisions

The criminal provisions of the original Clean Water Act were contained in Section 309(c). Section 309(c)(1) of the Clean Water Act provided misdemeanor penalties of up to one year of imprisonment and a $25,000 fine for "willful" or "negligent" violation of effluent limitations prescribed by the Act, or of conditions or limitations in NPDES permits issued by the EPA Administrator or a state in a Section 404 permit. The same act became a felony if it was committed "after a first conviction." [53]

Section 309(c)(2) of the original Clean Water Act established misdemeanor penalties of up to 6 months imprisonment and a $10,000 fine for knowingly making a false statement in any required document or the knowing falsification of records or tampering with monitoring devices "required to be maintained" under the Act.

---

[52]   *See* "More Prosecutions Under New Air Bill Predicted by Justice Department, EPA," 21 Environment Reporter (BNA) 421 (June 29, 1990).

[53]   Clean Water Act, Section 309(c)(1), 33 U.S.C. § 1319(c)(1) (1982).

3.1.2.B   Water Quality Act of 1987

In the Water Quality Act of 1987, Congress amended the Clean Water Act, adding new breadth to the Clean Water Act's criminal sanctions.[54] The penalties for a *negligent violation* of effluent limitations or violations of conditions or limitations in permits remained the same under the terms of an amended Section 309(c)(1). However, the *knowing violation* of permits or standards, as set forth under an amended Section 309(c)(2), was elevated to felony status. Both subsections provide criminal penalties for introducing into any publicly owned treatment works ("POTW") any pollutant or hazardous substance that the discharger knew or reasonably should have known could cause personal injury or possible damage or which would cause a POTW to violate its permit limits.

The Act also provides for the crime of "knowing endangerment" under Section 309(c)(3). That provision provides in pertinent part:

> Any person who knowingly violates section 1311, 1312, 1313, 1316, 1317, 1318, 1328, or 1345 of this title, or any permit condition [under Section 1342 or 1344] . . . and who knows at that time that he thereby places another person in imminent danger of death or serious bodily injury, shall, upon conviction, be subject to a fine of not more than $250,000 or imprisonment of not more than 15 years, or both.

---

[54]   Legislation to revise and re-authorize the Clean Water Act is likely to be addressed in the 103rd Congress. President Clinton has indicated that he will support new clean water legislation.

An organization convicted pursuant to section 309(c)(3) is subject to a maximum fine of $1,000,000. As with the other sections, the maximum fines for knowing endangerment double after a first conviction.

The enactment of a knowing endangerment provision is symptomatic of the changes affecting environmental crime statutes. The crime involves a knowing violation of an applicable permit, statute, rule or regulation by a person "who knows at that time that he thereby places another person in imminent danger of death or serious bodily injury." The language is similar to that contained in Section 3008(e) of RCRA.

The "knowing endangerment" requirement of Section 309(c)(3) was interpreted in the case of *United States v. Borowski*.[55] In *Borowski*, company officers directed employees to pour spent nickel plating baths and nitric acid baths into the sewer without any pretreatment and in violation of the pretreatment standards promulgated by EPA pursuant to the Clean Water Act. The company and its president were indicted and convicted of knowingly discharging the nickel baths into the sewer system and the POTW in violation of EPA's pretreatment standards and placing the company's employees in imminent danger of death or serious bodily injury.

---

[55] No. CR 89-256 WD (D. Mass. May 3, 1990), cited in 5 Toxics Law Reporter (BNA) 770 (Nov. 14, 1990).

The convictions were reversed on appeal based on the court's decision that the knowing endangerment requirement of § 309(c)(3) cannot be premised upon a danger that occurs before the pollutant reaches a POTW and before a violation of the statute occurs. The court held that the knowing endangerment must arise from a violation of the statute and that the endangerment to Borowski's employees' health was not dependent on such a violation.[56] The Court's holding is limited to the Clean Water Act. Specifically, the Court held that the Clean Water Act is limited in its purpose and, unlike RCRA, does not extend to the handling of pollutants or the protection of health.[57]

Section 312(c)(4) of the Clean Water Act also contains felony sanctions for anyone "who knowingly makes any false material statement . . . in any application, record, report, plan, or other document filed or required to be maintained under" the Act. Penalties for a first conviction are a maximum $10,000 fine or up to 2 years imprisonment, or both.

---

[56]   977 F.2d 27, 30 (1st Cir. 1992).

[57]   *Id.* at 31.

3.1.3 THE RESOURCE CONSERVATION AND RECOVERY ACT ("RCRA")

3.1.3.A   Criminal Provisions

RCRA prohibits certain treatment, storage, disposal or transportation of hazardous waste and provides criminal sanctions for violations in Section 3008(d). Sections 3008(d)(1) and (2), as recently amended, provide for felony penalties of up to 5 years imprisonment and/or fines up to $50,000 per day of violation for knowingly transporting hazardous waste to an unpermitted facility or for knowingly disposing of hazardous waste without a permit.[58]

Section 3008(d)(3) provides penalties of up to 2 years imprisonment and/or fines of up to $50,000 a day against any person who "knowingly omits material information or makes any false material statement" regarding records. Similar penalties are imposed under Section 3008(d)(4) for the knowing destruction or alteration of certain RCRA records. Penalties are imposed upon any person who "knowingly generates, stores, treats, transports, disposes of, exports, or otherwise handles [such hazardous waste] . . . and who knowingly destroys, alters, conceals, or fails to file any record, application, manifest, report or other document required to be maintained or filed."

---

[58]   Previously the penalties for Sections 3008(d)(1) and (2) had been prison up to 2 years and/or fines up to $ 50,000 per day of the violation.

3.1.3.B   "Knowing Endangerment"

The 1980 amendment to RCRA, as further amended in 1984, led to the creation of Section 3008(e), which provides:

> Any person who knowingly transports, treats, stores, disposes of, or exports any hazardous waste . . . in violation of paragraph (1), (2), (3), (4), (5), (6), or (7) of subsection (d) of this section who knows at that time that he thereby places another person in imminent danger of death or serious bodily injury, shall, upon conviction, be subject to a fine of not more than $250,000 or imprisonment for not more than 15 years, or both. A defendant that is an organization shall . . . be subject to a fine of not more than $1,000,000.

The use of the "knowing endangerment" offense as a serious prosecutorial tool against corporate violators was demonstrated in the case of *United States v. Protex Industries*.[59] There the corporation was convicted of knowingly endangering three employees who worked in the company's drum recycling facility and were exposed to hazardous substances. Initially, the corporation was fined $7.53 million. However, all but $440,000 of the fine was ultimately suspended on the condition that the company pay almost $1 million restitution and $2.1 million in cleanup costs.

---

[59]   874 F.2d 740 (10th Cir. 1989).

3.1.4 REPORTING VIOLATIONS UNDER CERCLA AND EPCRA

Congress added to the list of environmental crimes by enacting the Superfund Amendment and Reauthorization Act of 1986 ("SARA"), which increased the penalties for criminal activities under the Comprehensive Environmental Response Compensation Liability Act ("CERCLA").

CERCLA, as amended by SARA, contains felony provisions with criminal fines of up to $250,000 for individuals ($500,000 for organizations) and sentences of up to 3 years for certain recordkeeping and reporting violations.[60] The filing of false CERCLA claims also has been criminalized, with equally strong felony provisions applying.[61]

Enacted as Title III of SARA, the Emergency Planning & Community Right-to-Know Act ("EPCRA") contains extensive reporting requirements for persons handling a wide range of chemicals. Criminal penalties are provided for failure to comply with EPCRA Section 304, which requires owners and operators of facilities to provide immediate notice of certain releases of hazardous substances to state and

---

[60]   Prison terms of up to 5 years may be imposed after a first conviction. *See* CERCLA Section 103(d)(2), 42 U.S.C. § 9603(d)(2) (falsifying and destruction of records required to be kept per EPA regulations); SARA, Section 325 (offense of falsifying or refusing emergency information under Emergency Planning & Community Right-to-Know Act of 1986).

[61]   CERCLA Section 112(b)(1), 42 U.S.C. § 9612(b)(1) (punishment of false claims knowingly submitted for reimbursement from the fund).

local emergency planning units. Section 325(b)(4) of EPCRA provides for criminal penalties for violation of Section 304:

> Any person who knowingly and willfully fails to provide notice in accordance with section [304] shall, upon conviction, be fined not more than $25,000 or imprisoned for not more than two years, or both (or in the case of a second or subsequent conviction, shall be fined not more than $50,000 or imprisoned for not more than five years, or both).

While no criminal enforcement cases have been decided under EPCRA, there are a number of CERCLA criminal cases. For example, in *United States v. Greer*[62] the court affirmed a conviction for failure to report a release of hazardous substances under CERCLA.

3.1.5   REGULATION OF CHEMICALS AND OTHER FEDERAL STATUTES

3.1.5.A.   The Federal Insecticide Fungicide and Rodenticide Act ("FIFRA")

FIFRA regulates registration, branding and other aspects of insecticides and similar substances. Section 14(b) of FIFRA establishes criminal penalties for the knowing violation of any provision of the Act.

---

[62]   850 F.2d 1447 (11th Cir. 1988).

While FIFRA penalties are more limited than those in other statutes, including only misdemeanor provisions, Congress has provided for criminal liability to be imposed vicariously upon a principal for "the act, omission, or failure of any officer, agent, or employee." No actual knowledge or culpable mental state is required of the principal.[63] Furthermore, in *United States v. Corbin Farm Service*[64], the court held that persons "using" a pesticide included persons who advised the applicator in its selection and application.

EPA's Office of Compliance Monitoring has indicated publicly that FIFRA is the emphasis of a new initiative at EPA. The prevalence at laboratories of criminal data fraud has encouraged EPA to start focusing more enforcement efforts on laboratory practices.[65]

3.1.5.B   The Toxic Substances Control Act ("TSCA")

Like FIFRA, TSCA is a statutory scheme that was enacted to regulate certain toxic substances. Its criminal enforcement provision applies to violations of Section 15 and carries misdemeanor penalties. Section 15 proscribes: the failure

---

[63]   Section 14(b)(4) (employee's act "also deemed to be the act" of principal).

[64]   444 F. Supp. 510, (E.D. Cal.), *affirmed*, 578 F.2d 259 (9th Cir. 1978).

[65]   "EPA Official Predicts Stepped-Up Effort on Good Laboratory Practices Enforcement," Daily Report for Executives, June 18, 1992, at A-21.

to comply with notice and handling restrictions, the use of substances processed negligently in violation of these restrictions, the failure to maintain proper records, and the refusal to allow regulatory inspections.[66] The penalties are fines of up to $25,000 per day of violations and/or up to one year imprisonment.

3.1.5.C   The Occupational Safety and Health Act ("OSHA"): Criminal Penalty Reform

OSHA provides only weak criminal penalties.[67] The history of OSHA criminal prosecution appears to be very limited. For example, OSHA provides only misdemeanor sanctions for willful violations that lead to the death of an employee. Since OSHA's inception at the end of 1970, nearly 200,000 workers have been killed in workplace accidents. However, only one employer has been jailed. That conviction occurred in 1989 and resulted in a 45 day prison sentence. From 1971 through 1990, OSHA referred only 74 cases to the Department of Justice for possible criminal action. There were 15 convictions out of the 20 cases prosecuted.

---

[66]   7 U.S.C. § 2614.

[67]   29 U.S.C. § 666(e).

3.1.5.D   Other Federal Statutes and Continuing Attention to Environmental Crimes in Federal Statutes

Congress is continually considering new bills that would increase the stringency of existing laws. For example, a recent bill proposed adding the "knowing violation" language of the Clean Water Act to CERCLA, FIFRA, the Ocean Dumping Act, the Safe Drinking Water Act, TSCA, and EPCRA; imposing strict contractor listing provisions; and preventing convicted persons from obtaining government contracts for performance at the violating facility until the EPA certifies that the violation has been remedied.

3.2   GENERAL CRIMINAL STATUTES

The government has been bold and creative in its use of other, somewhat obscure criminal statutes. For example, in the case of the Exxon Valdez spill,[68/] the government included charges based on the Migratory Bird Treaty Act for the killing of migratory birds without a permit. As the Federal enforcement climate becomes more aggressive, prosecutors are using general criminal provisions in order to seek stiffer criminal penalties.

Typical of this trend is the government's use of the Federal conspiracy

---

[68/]   *United States v. Exxon*, No. A90-015 (D. Alaska filed Feb. 27, 1990).

statute.[69] In *United States v. Levy*[70] the president and supervisor of a drum recycling company were charged with conspiracy as well as violations of RCRA storage and disposal and Clean Water Act provisions. Similarly, in *United States v. EKOTEK Inc.*,[71] conspiracy was added to Clean Water Act, Clean Air Act and RCRA violations in order to seek stiffer penalties. Prosecutors also have used other general criminal provisions in environmental cases including Federal laws criminalizing false statements, mail and wire fraud, and aiding and abetting. The false statements offense (which consists of knowingly and willfully falsifying, concealing or covering up a material fact or making any false fictitious or fraudulent statements) attracts fines of up to $10,000 and/or prison terms up to 5 years under 18 U.S.C. § 1001. It was used in *United States v. Rudd*,[72] an environmental case where the government alleged that the supplier of laboratory items falsified control

---

[69]   A conspiracy is simply an agreement, express or implied, for two or more persons to act in concert to violate the law. The penalty for conspiracy under 18 U.S.C. § 371 is as follows: "each [conspirator] shall be fined not more than $10,000 or imprisoned not more than five years, or both. If, however, the offense, the commission of which is the object of the conspiracy, is a misdemeanor only, the punishment for such conspiracy shall not exceed the maximum punishment provided for such misdemeanor."

[70]   *See* 21 Environment Reporter (BNA) 824 (Aug. 24, 1990).

[71]   *See* 21 Environment Reporter (BNA) 423 (June 29, 1990).

[72]   No. 90-0630 (N.D. Cal. filed Nov. 30, 1990).

data submitted to the EPA. It was also used in *United States v. YWC Inc.*,[73] regarding false reports sent to EPA concerning CERCLA test results.

3.3   THE CRIMINAL FINES IMPROVEMENTS ACT OF 1987

Fines for all offenses, including environmental crimes, are subject to an alternative maximum fine under the Criminal Fines Improvement Act of 1987. Under the applicable portion of that Act, the maximum fine for any offense by an individual is "the greatest of:

> (1) the amount specified in the law setting forth the offense;
>
> (2) the applicable amount under subsection (d) of [Section 3571];
>
> (3) for a felony, not more than $250,000;
>
> (4) for a misdemeanor resulting in death, not more than $250,000; [or]
>
> (5) for a Class A misdemeanor that does not result in death, not more than $100,000 . . . ."[74]

Organizational fines are calculated similarly, but the fines are doubled. Perhaps the most important provision, however, applicable to individuals and to organizations, is section 3571(d), which provides an alternative fine as follows:

> If any person derives pecuniary gain from the offense, or if

---

[73]   No. B90-64-WWE (D. Conn. Dec. 5, 1990), *cited in* 21 Environment Reporter (BNA) 1565 (Dec. 14, 1990).

[74]   18 U.S.C. § 3571(b).

the offense results in pecuniary loss to a person other than
the defendant, the defendant may be fined not more than the
greater of twice the gross gain or twice the gross loss . . . .
[75]

These harsh provisions are only inapplicable when a statute excludes their use "by

specific reference."[76]

---

[75]   18 U.S.C. § 3571(d).

[76]   18 U.S.C. § 3571(e).

CHAPTER 4

**ASSESSING THE COSTS AND RISKS OF USING
ENVIRONMENTAL AUDITS TO IDENTIFY AND CORRECT VIOLATIONS**

4.1   GOVERNMENT ENCOURAGEMENT OF AUDITS

In 1986, EPA issued a policy statement encouraging the use of audits to help regulated companies comply with environmental laws and identify and correct violations.[77] EPA enforcement policy was to consider "on a case-by-case basis," the honest and genuine efforts of regulated entities to avoid and promptly correct violations and underlying environmental problems.

EPA enforcement settlements appear to favor environmental auditing. In addition to encouraging the development of corporate auditing programs, EPA has promoted administrative, civil and criminal settlements that require ongoing environmental audits. EPA has broad authority to negotiate an audit provision in a consent decree as part of its authority to require self-monitoring as a remedy for violators.[78]

In its Report on 1992 enforcement actions, EPA listed for the first time Supplemental Environmental Projects (SEPs). EPA listed 409 SEPs in its

---

[77]   *See* EPA, *Environmental Auditing Policy Statement*, 51 Fed. Reg. 25004 (July 9, 1986).

[78]   *See* Clean Water Act § 308, 33 U.S.C. § 1318; Clean Air Act § 114, 42 U.S.C. § 7414.

Report, estimating their value at $50.1 million. SEPs are non-monetary

components of enforcement actions wherein parties agree to take certain actions

in return for a reduction in the dollar amount of a penalty. SEPs include

pollution prevention, pollution reduction, environmental restoration,

environmental auditing and public awareness projects.

On July 1, 1991, the Department of Justice issued a policy statement

concerning environmental audits. The statement provided:

> It is the policy of the Department of Justice to encourage self-
> auditing, self-policing and voluntary disclosure of
> environmental violations by the regulated community by
> indicating that these activities are viewed as mitigating factors
> in the Department's exercise of criminal environmental
> enforcement discretion. This document is intended to describe
> the factors that the Department of Justice considers in
> deciding whether to bring a criminal prosecution for a
> violation of an environmental statute, so that such prosecutions
> do not create a disincentive to or undermine the goal of
> encouraging critical self-auditing, self-policing and voluntary
> disclosure.[29]

The statement was designed to encourage self-auditing by giving the regulated

community a sense of certain factors that influence prosecutorial discretion. An

environmental audit is viewed by the Department of Justice as an important part

---

[29] *See* U.S. Department of Justice, *Factors in Decisions on Criminal Prosecutions for
Environmental Violations in the Context of Significant Voluntary Compliance or Disclosure Efforts
by the Violator* (July 1, 1991). The Department of Justice's Policy Statement is set forth in full in
Appendix C to this Guide.

of a larger compliance program.

The government's call for self-auditing and voluntary disclosure as a way to reduce the likelihood of criminal enforcement actions has met with mixed results. Criminal prosecutions are not ruled out categorically, and fears exist regarding civil enforcement actions. For example, when an AMOCO facility received a $5 million civil penalty recently, industry representatives complained that self-audit information was used in the enforcement action. EPA officials denied that the voluntarily disclosed information was linked to the action, but they recognized that any appearance of a tie could serve as a disincentive to self-audits.[80]

In May 1992, the EPA Assistant Administrator for Enforcement stated that he knew of no cases in which voluntary disclosure of self-audit information had led to criminal prosecution and that only information from audits obtained by subpoena had yielded criminal prosecutions.[81] A Department of Justice official, however, has stated that an audit and disclosure is not enough. The Department of Justice has taken the position that they must see a commitment to cleanup and efforts to solve problems uncovered by audits before they will

---

[80] "Fines at Pilot Plant Scare Industry Off New EPA Voluntary Compliance Plan," Inside EPA Weekly Report, June 12, 1992, at 1.

[81] "Companies' Fear of Environmental Disclosure Has No Basis, Top EPA Enforcement Official Says," 23 Environment Reporter (BNA) 24 (May 1, 1992).

decline to prosecute.[82] The draft Federal Sentencing Guidelines for sentencing

organizations convicted of environmental crimes similarly propose to reward

environmental audit programs that are designed and implemented with sufficient

authority, personnel and other resources.

Courts have included audit requirements in sentences imposed on

corporations. Unichem Corporation, in addition to being fined $1.5 million for

three felony violations under RCRA, was sentenced to probation that required

its engineers to conduct an environmental audit at certain facilities.

New Jersey's Environmental Prosecutor's Office has published Voluntary

Environmental Audit/Compliance Guidelines to encourage and recognize

voluntary compliance audit programs adopted by New Jersey businesses and

industry.[83] The stated goal of the guidelines is: (i) to give prosecutors

direction in the exercise of prosecutorial discretion; and (ii) to give New Jersey

business and industry a sense of what to expect from the decision-making process

in the exercise of prosecutorial discretion in criminal matters when a

compliance/audit program is implemented. The New Jersey guidelines contain

an illustrative, but not exclusive, list of factors prosecutors will consider in

---

[82]   *See* 22 Environment Reporter (BNA) 2406, 2407 (Feb. 21, 1992).

[83]   Robert J. Del Tufo and Steven J. Madonna, *New Jersey Voluntary Environmental Audit/Compliance Guidelines* (May 15, 1992). A complete copy of the guidelines is included in Appendix B of this Guide.

determining such matters as whether to initiate criminal prosecution, the nature of the charges, the timing of the prosecution and the defendants charged. The factors identified in the New Jersey guidelines are:

- Existence and scope of the environmental compliance/audit program;

- Maintenance, inspection and operation features;

- Adoption and promotion of the compliance/audit program by management;

- Adequacy of formal employee training;

- Adequacy of funding, personnel and resources;

- Involvement of qualified independent professionals;

- Existence of periodic audit requirements;

- Existence of policies and practices regarding correction, modification or remediation;

- Existence of employee disciplinary policies and practices;

- Existence of employee recognition and reward policies and practices;

- Existence and pervasiveness of non-compliance;

- Occurrence of voluntary disclosure; and

- Extent of company cooperation.

4.2   COSTS AND RISKS OF ENVIRONMENTAL AUDITS

Notwithstanding the clear benefits of environmental audits, there are a number of risks. First, once a violation is discovered, the company and its management may face the risk of criminal or civil prosecution until and unless the violation is corrected. Secondly, risk arises when an audit produces findings which must be reported to environmental agencies under Federal, state or local reporting statutes.

Corporations may preclude such sanctions if their disclosures and cooperation are voluntary, timely and complete as suggested by the July 1991 Justice Department statement. If the government makes any independent discovery of a violation prior to disclosure, it is unlikely that a corporation will meet with prosecutorial leniency.

4.3   THE COMPLIANCE DIAGNOSTIC

A prudent first step to establishing a compliance program is a compliance diagnostic. Such a first step can provide an evaluation of policies, programs and problems and serve as a basis for further actions such as in-depth audits.

A compliance diagnostic allows a company to investigate, mitigate or otherwise address serious compliance issues before opening its doors to outside

consulting firms or to a full-blown internal audit. A phased compliance

diagnostic allows a corporation to make informed decisions about compliance

issues and priorities while avoiding the unforeseen and often unfortunate

consequences of a full-speed-ahead, unfocused, undisciplined, compliance audit.

A compliance diagnostic can provide a broad, critical evaluation and overview of

compliance problems for consideration by management. It should look for both

systemic and episodic weaknesses. The initial focus of a compliance diagnostic

should involve the identification of activities which can lead to or reduce

significant liabilities. The next phase should involve limited distribution of a

privileged report to management. The report should identify potential liabilities,

areas requiring further scrutiny and management options.

The strategy and approach to an environmental diagnostic should include

the following elements:

I.   **PURPOSE AND OBJECTIVES**

- A critical evaluation of environmental programs and problems for consideration by management.

- An evaluation which maximizes attorney-client and self-assessment privileges and looks for both systemic and episodic weaknesses.

- An evaluation which provides management with an evaluation upon which management can decide to investigate further, to mitigate, or to otherwise address identified deficiencies.

II. INITIAL FOCUS OF A COMPLIANCE DIAGNOSTIC

- Seek to identify activities which can lead to or reduce significant liabilities such as:

  - Lawsuits or other claims;

  - Agency actions undertaken or contemplated; and

  - Recovery from insurance or other responsible entities.

- Evaluate management of environmental programs including:

  - Organization and function of environmental protection programs;

  - Assimilation of information received by the company (information in); and

  - Procedures for submitting reports to government agencies (information out).

- Assess operations and program implementation by:

  - Determining regulatory and compliance status;

  - Reviewing the mechanics of document preparation and signatory authority; and

  - Managing and tracking compliance requirements, paperwork, permits, manifests, etc.

III. NEXT PHASE

- Report to management on findings, including description of issues, potential liabilities, areas needing further scrutiny, management options, and operational status.

- Initiate follow-up actions, perhaps including a formal audit program conducted by company personnel or by an outside firm; and

- Advise management on the implementation of actions to solve identified problems, and evaluate the operation of any audit program.

NUTS AND BOLTS

Scope of the Phased Environmental Diagnostic

An environmental diagnostic is a process that adapts to the information collected during its early stages. Early efforts to collect and review preliminary background materials can expedite and streamline the process.

Collection and Review of Background Materials

As a general matter, the following documents should be collected and reviewed first:

- Organization charts;

- Facility site plans;

- Environmental permits issued by Federal, state or local agencies (including summary monitoring data related to such permits);

- Documents relating to violations of Federal, state or local environmental laws, rules or regulations;

- Documents filed under Federal, state or local laws, concerning the release of pollutants or hazardous materials into the environment;

- Copies of reports resulting from government inspections regarding environmental issues;

- Documents filed in compliance with Title III of SARA (Emergency Planning and Community Right-to- Know Act) or similar statutes;

- Notifications that a facility is a generator of hazardous waste, including notices under Section 3010 of the Resource Conservation and Recovery Act;

- Manifests reflecting the off-site shipment of hazardous wastes;

- A list of off-site treatment or disposal facilities (including municipal landfills) to which hazardous and non-hazardous wastes have been sent;

- Any notifications that the company is or may be a potentially responsible party under the Comprehensive Environmental Response, Compensation, and Liability Act;

- Copies of Material Safety Data Sheets for all chemicals utilized by all facilities;

- Copies of any compliance orders, consent order judgments, waivers or variances that have been issued to the company under any environmental or health and safety regulatory program;

- Registrations or documents identifying underground and above-ground storage tanks; and

- Copies of internal audit reports or reports produced by outside consultants concerning any environmental or health and safety issues at company facilities.

Site Assessments - A number of company facilities should be selected for site assessments. The assessments involve interviews with appropriate personnel, reviews of operations, reviews of records, and site inspections.

Review of Agency Records - A search should be performed of agency environmental records concerning company facilities, and, where appropriate, records concerning disposal facilities used by the company.

Contracts with Waste Haulers and Disposal Facilities - Where appropriate, companies which transport, recycle, or dispose of wastes from company facilities may need to be contacted.

4.4 PROTECTING CONFIDENTIALITY OF DIAGNOSTIC/AUDIT INFORMATION

The auditing process may create documentation that is or should be regarded as subject to attorney-client privilege or other privileges. The following steps should be taken to preserve the attorney-client privilege:

- Before the audit begins, the chairman of the board or other high-ranking corporate officer should write to counsel conducting the audit to request legal advice concerning the corporation's present compliance with environmental laws, and changes that can be made to increase compliance and reduce the corporation's risk in any potential legal proceedings. The letter should stress that the investigation to be conducted is to provide management with information, not otherwise available to it, to promote these goals, and that the investigation and legal advice are to remain highly confidential.

- Counsel should confirm, by letter, the same points.

- Counsel should segregate activity on the environmental audit from any other activity on behalf of the corporation, especially activities that might be characterized as related to business advice.

- The chairman of the board or other high-ranking officer should send a memorandum to all corporate employees stating that the audit will be performed, and instructing employees to cooperate fully. Counsel should be identified. The memorandum should stress that the purpose is to provide management with legal advice concerning environmental compliance, in order to promote the corporation's policy of complying with all applicable environmental laws and regulations. The memorandum also should state that all communications with counsel during the course of the audit are privileged and confidential.

- At the outset of each employee's interview, counsel should repeat the same points from the corporation's memorandum. It may be advisable to secure the employee's written acknowledgement that he or she understands the nature and purpose of the interview, and the need for strict confidentiality. No third party should be present during the interview except when essential for the interview to go forward (*e.g.*, a translator). If a third party's presence is essential, the need for this presence should be documented, and the third party should be pledged to confidentiality. The employee should not take notes during the interview.

- Counsel's report to management should be marked as privileged and confidential. It should show clearly the *legal* nature of the advice rendered; thus, rather than report raw interview results, it should analyze the results of the factual investigation under applicable legal standards. The rationale for any recommended changes should be explicitly legal, rather than for business purposes.

- Confidentiality of diagnostic/audit results must be maintained within the corporation's files. The results should be segregated from non-legal material. Access should be defined and limited. Results should not be publicized.

CHAPTER 5

PROTECTING YOURSELF WHEN WORKING WITH
OUTSIDE CONTRACTORS: CONTRACT TIPS AND PITFALLS

5.1   INTRODUCTION

Today, environmental contractors and consultants are more involved than

ever in the daily environmental compliance activities of U.S. companies.

Although much of this work is related to routine regulatory matters and site

remediation, there are a number of areas in which contractors may become

involved in activities related to potential criminal liability. The purpose of this

chapter is to describe the possible roles for environmental contractors in the

area of criminal liability and to suggest specific contract language that can be

used to protect your company when negotiating contracts with such contractors.

5.2   THE ROLE OF THE ENVIRONMENTAL CONTRACTOR

There are a number of steps during the development and defense of a

criminal investigation in which a contractor may play a significant role.

- First, a company may choose to include a contractor in the team
  performing an environmental audit of the company to identify
  potential civil and criminal liabilities. A contractor who
  understands the technical aspects of the company's processes may
  be particularly useful in talking with employees about their jobs
  and compliance activities.

- If potential liability is discovered, the company may include an environmental consultant in its internal team to investigate the possible wrongdoing. For example, scientific and technical consultants may be useful in assisting counsel in evaluating technical documents relating to the case.

- Once a grand jury investigation is underway, the company may find it useful to hire an outside scientific expert to assist in preparing witnesses for testifying, *e.g.*, by making sure the witnesses have a clear understanding of the technical aspects of the company's compliance with environmental regulations.

- If an indictment is returned, a consultant may be helpful in assisting counsel in determining the extent to which the technical and scientific facts support the indictment, and may serve as expert witnesses in the trial.

5.3   CONTRACTS WITH ENVIRONMENTAL CONTRACTORS AND CONSULTANTS

5.3.A   General Advice

Companies wishing to hire an environmental contractor or consultant for any purpose should carefully consider the nature of the work to be performed and the potential liabilities that may be associated with the work. Although normally the contractor will present the company with its standard contract, be wary of suggestions that the standard contract provisions are sufficient for the project at hand.

Likewise, one should not assume that the meanings of words used in the contract are a given. Words and phrases with regulatory significance (*e.g.*, "hazardous substance", "discharge") should be defined as clearly and comprehensively as possible.

In negotiating a contract the goal is to avoid future disputes and possible litigation regarding the meaning of the contract. Attempt to anticipate areas of dispute and spell out clearly the parties' intents and understandings.

In many situations, particularly where possible criminal liability is involved, it may be advisable to have the environmental contractor contract with counsel rather than with the company. In this way, reports and other documents prepared by the contractor may be protected from discovery.[84/]

Finally, a consultant should be selected based on its reputation and skill for a particular chore (*e.g.*, environmental auditing, litigation support) rather than on its general reputation.

[84/]   *See, e.g., State ex rel. Corbin v. Ybarra*, 777 P.2d 686, 692, 161 Ariz. 188 (Ariz. 1989) (environmental engineer's report prepared at instruction of outside counsel in connection with pending criminal charges protected under attorney work product doctrine from unauthorized use by state in grand jury proceeding).

5.3.B SPECIFIC CONTRACT ISSUES

5.3.B.1 Standard of Care

The contract should establish the standard of care to which the contractor

will be held. Some examples of standard of care provisions are:

> The Contractor agrees that the work it performs shall be done in
> accordance with good and sound professional practices and
> procedures, consistent with that level of care currently observed by
> other experienced, knowledgeable and duly skilled members of the
> Contractor's profession working under similar conditions.

> OR

> The Contractor will perform services in accordance with generally
> accepted practices of environmental professionals undertaking
> similar services in the same locale under like or identical
> circumstances.

These clauses establish an expert, rather than a "reasonable man," standard, but

connote an average generally accepted standard of care, not a standard based on

the state-of-the-art scientific knowledge or best technical expertise reasonably

available.

In addition, the contract should establish that the work will be performed

in a manner consistent with all applicable laws and regulatory requirements. For

example:

> All activities undertaken by the Contractor to complete this work
> shall be in accordance with the requirements of the Scope of

Work, and all applicable law, including relevant state and Federal laws and regulations, in effect in the jurisdiction in which the work is performed.

5.3.B.2 Exclusive Use Provision

An Exclusive Use provision will help to limit the possibility of contract claims of third parties. A example of such a provision is:

The Company agrees that the Contractor's services are on behalf of and for the exclusive use of the Company for the purposes set forth in the Contract.

5.3.B.3 Independent Contractor Status

It is often useful to expressly spell out the relationship between the company and the contractor in the contract. For example:

It is expressly understood that the Contractor is an independent contractor and that neither the Contractor not its employees or subcontractors are servants, agents, employees or representatives of the Company. The Company shall not be held to be a party to any subcontract entered into by the Contractor to perform the work required by this Contract.

In addition to clearly delineating the parties' relationship for purposes of the contract and related contracts, such a contract provision may also provide some protection to the company if the contractor or a subcontractor engages in criminal activity during its performance of the contract, by making it less likely that a prosecutor would find the company liable for the actions of the contractor or subcontractor.

5.3.B.4 Approval of Subcontractors

The company can obtain control over the quality and number of subcontractors used by the contractor by providing in the contract that the company must approve the use of any subcontractor for performance of the contract. For example:

> Before contracting with any subcontractors, the Contractor shall notify the Company of the particular subcontractor and obtain the written approval of the Company to hire the subcontractor.

5.3.B.5 Indemnification

Indemnification provisions are often the most difficult part of the contract to negotiate. Ideally, the indemnification clause will define clearly the scope of the indemnification, the longevity of the indemnification (*i.e.*, whether it survives the completion of the contract activities), and the trigger for invoking the indemnification clause (*e.g.*, incurring costs, the receipt of a formal administrative order, etc.).

The standard contracts presented by contractors often contain language providing that the company will indemnify the contractor for all liabilities other than those caused by the contractor's gross negligence or willful misconduct.

Such indemnification provisions are rarely acceptable to companies. An example

of an indemnification clause that is more protective of the company is the

following:

> The Contractor shall indemnify and hold harmless the Company from and against all claims, damages, losses, judgments and expenses, including, but not limited to, reasonable attorney's fees, arising out of the Contractor's performance of services under the Contract, except for the exclusions listed below. In the event that claims, damages, losses, judgments and expenses, including, but not limited to, reasonable attorney's fees, are caused by the Company's sole negligence, the Company shall fully indemnify, hold harmless, and defend the Contractor. In the event the claims, damages, losses, judgments and expenses, including, but not limited to, reasonable attorney's fees, are the result of the negligence of both the Company and the Contractor or its subcontractor, the Company and the Contractor shall be liable to the extent or degree of their respective negligence, as determined by mutual agreement or as determined by adjudication of comparative negligence.

> Hazardous Waste Exclusion -- For services involving or relating to hazardous waste elements of this Contract [which should be defined elsewhere in the contract], it is further agreed that the Company shall indemnify and hold harmless the Contractor and its consultants, agents and employees from and against all claims, damages, losses and expenses, including, but not limited to, reasonable attorney's fees, arising out of or resulting from the performance of the work by the Contractor, or claims against the Contractor arising from the work of others, related to hazardous waste. This exclusion does not apply to the extent any such claims are due to the Contractor's (i) breach of its obligations under this Contract; (ii) negligence; (iii) willful misconduct; or (iv) "professional services" performed in the design and construction of treatment facilities.

5.3.B.6 Limitations of Liability

Contractors normally will seek to have included in their contracts clauses limiting their liability to the sums paid by the client to the contractor under the contract. The limitations of liability will provide that the contractor shall not be liable for any special, indirect, punitive or consequential damages of any kind. The provision may also require that any claim under the contract must be brought within a specific time period, such as one year.

Although it is difficult to negotiate a contract without such a limitation of liability, sometimes a contractor will agree to a higher limit of liability (above the sums paid under the contract) or will allow the company to purchase additional professional liability insurance for a premium. The time for bringing claims may also be extended through negotiation. As an alternative, the contract could include a provision such as the following:

> Except for bodily injury and property damage, no party shall be liable for any indirect, exemplary, punitive, incidental or consequential damages.

5.3.B.7 Major Changes and Delays

Companies should include in their contracts with environmental contractors language that clearly sets forth how major changes to the work or delays in the performance of the work will be handled by the parties. For example:

> "Major changes" are defined as those that would affect the cost of the work to the Company, those that would require amendment of the Scope of Work, or those that would delay completion of the work beyond the applicable deadlines. Major changes shall not be made except upon the written approval of the Company. The amount of any additional or lesser compensation shall be negotiated by the Parties on either a lump-sum or time and materials basis.

> The Contractor shall not be entitled to compensation for increased costs due to delays unless caused by the Company or by force majeure [which should be defined elsewhere in the contract]. In the event that the Contractor believes that it will incur increased costs due to a significant delay caused by the Company or force majeure, the Contractor shall immediately notify the Company, in writing, specifying the incremental cost of the delay. The Company will negotiate with the Contractor with respect to the cost impacts that the Contractor must incur. The Contractor shall make every effort to mitigate any damages caused by such delay.

5.3.B.8 Condition of the Site

Where a contract involves field work by the contractor, the contract should expressly provide that the company is not responsible for any injury to the contractor's employees and subcontractors. Suggested language would be as follows:

> The Company makes no warranty as to the condition of the Site, or as to any health hazards that might exist there. The Contractor assumes all responsibility for the health, safety and welfare of all persons who may be assigned by the Contractor or its subcontractors, and for any liabilities that may arise therefrom.

5.3.B.9 Disposal of Wastes

Where the contractor will take samples or otherwise produce wastes at a site, the contract should provide for who is responsible for disposal of those wastes. For example:

> The Contractor shall be responsible for the disposal of wastes, including, but not limited to, samples and drilling fluids, resulting from the Contractor's and its subcontractors' activities. All such wastes shall be removed from the site by the Contractor for proper disposal in accordance with all applicable federal, state and local laws, ordinances and regulations.

5.3.B.10 Insurance

The company should make sure that the Contractor has adequate insurance to cover its activities under the contract. This insurance should go beyond mere comprehensive general liability insurance. The following provision includes some of the types of insurance that should be required in the contract:

> The Contractor certifies that it currently has, and shall maintain in effect throughout the term of this Contract, the following insurance:
>
> (a) Worker's Compensation and Employer's Liability Insurance in accordance with the laws of [state];
> (b) Comprehensive General Liability Insurance, including Contractual Liability:
> Bodily Injury Liability -- $1,000,000 each person; $1,000,000 each accident

Property Damage Liability -- $1,000,000 each accident;
$1,000,000 aggregate

(c)   Automobile Liability insurance -- combined single limit for bodily injury and property damage in the amount of $1,000,000;

(d)   Umbrella policy in the amount of $2,000,000 which shall provide coverage in excess of the underlying coverage described in subparagraphs (a) through (c) above; and

(e)   Architects and Engineers Professional Liability Insurance in the amount of $2,000,000 per loss (act or omission or series of acts or omissions) and aggregate limit.

5.3.B.11 Key Personnel

If the contractor has stated that a particular person or persons will be involved in the work under the contract, or if it is important to the company that particular persons manage the work, expressly provide in the contract:

The key individuals identified herein are considered essential to the work being performed under this Contract and critical to the grant of this work to the Contractor. Therefore substitutions for such personnel or substantial reductions in their efforts shall not be made without the prior written consent of the Company. [NAME] shall be the Contractor's designated Project Manager and [NAME] shall be the Contractor's designated Assistant Project Manager.

5.3.B.12 Laboratories

In order to assure that the contractor uses a reputable and accredited laboratory in connection with the work performed under the contract, it is useful to provide a paragraph such as the following:

Those laboratories which the Contractor uses to perform services related to this Contract shall be appropriately certified pursuant to applicable Federal, state and local laws, ordinances and regulations. In the event that any such laboratory loses its certification during the term of this Contract, the Contractor shall immediately notify the Company of such loss of certification, shall select another certified laboratory, and shall send new samples, if necessary, to the replacement laboratory.

5.3.B.13 Retention and Confidentiality of Records

The contract should specify how long the contractor must retain records relating to the work under the contract and should require the contractor to treat the records as confidential. For example:

The Contractor shall maintain records and documents relating to performance of the work hereunder for at least ten years after the work is completed.

The Contractor shall consider the work performed hereunder and the results of any testing performed hereunder as confidential and as proprietary to the Company. Except to the extent required by law, or by a court order, the Contractor shall not without the prior written consent of the Company: (1) publish or otherwise divulge any information whatsoever concerning the work under the contract irrespective of the source of such information; or (2) discuss with anyone other than the Company the nature of the work the Contractor is performing hereunder.

In the event the Contractor (or anyone to whom confidential information is furnished by the Contractor) becomes legally compelled to disclose any confidential information, the Contractor will provide the Company with prompt written notice so that the Company may seek a protective order or other appropriate remedy.

5.3.B.14 Warranty of Non-Disbarment

The company should get a warranty from the contractor that it is not

currently disbarred by EPA. For example:

> The Contractor warrants that it is not currently disbarred or
> suspended by EPA pursuant to 40 C.F.R. Part 32, nor has
> knowledge of a threatened or pending disbarment or suspension.

5.4   CONCLUSION

Because the ramifications of contractual language can be so far-reaching,

it always makes sense to have your company's contracts reviewed by attorneys

familiar with environmental liability and contracting issues. Substantial

problems, as well as insubstantial headaches, can be avoided by paying extra

attention to the details up front.

CHAPTER 6

HOW REGULATORS PICK THEIR TARGETS
FOR ENVIRONMENTAL CRIMINAL PROSECUTION

6.1   INTRODUCTION

A prosecutor's decision to bring a criminal enforcement action under one of the environmental statutes is a complex one. Although some cases, such as those involving midnight dumping, cry out for criminal prosecution, in many cases a significant amount of discretion is involved in determining whether a violation of a statute should be civilly or criminally enforced.[85/] Because the impacts of these decisions are so critical to the regulated community, prudent corporate management should require corporate officers to learn as much as they can about the factors affecting the exercise of that discretion and to take whatever steps are possible to avoid becoming the target of a criminal action.

This chapter discusses the factors considered by U.S. Department of Justice attorneys in deciding whether to criminally prosecute environmental noncompliance, other factors that may affect the exercise of prosecutorial discretion, and steps a company can take to reduce the likelihood of being a target of criminal enforcement.

[85/]   "[T]he reach of the criminal sanction is extremely broad and the threshold of culpability is unusually low, allowing for considerable overlap between the civil and criminal cases and thus a heavy dependence on judgment calls." G.S. Anderson, "Exercising Prosecutorial Discretion: Civil vs. Criminal Enforcement of Environmental Violations -- What Policies?" C617 ALI-ABA 7 (April 11, 1991).

6.2   DEPARTMENT OF JUSTICE GUIDANCE

The U.S. Department of Justice has issued an internal guidance document titled *Factors in Decisions on Criminal Prosecutions for Environmental Violations in the Context of Significant Voluntary Compliance or Disclosure Efforts by the Violator* (July 1, 1991).[86] Although this document is intended only to provide guidance to Department of Justice lawyers deciding whether to bring criminal charges against an environmental violator, it also serves to educate the regulated community about how to reduce the possibility that a criminal action will be brought.[87]

The Department of Justice guidance lists six factors that the Department will consider in deciding whether to pursue a criminal enforcement action:

- Voluntary disclosure

- Cooperation

- Preventive measures and compliance programs

- Pervasiveness of noncompliance

- Internal disciplinary action

- Subsequent compliance efforts.

---

[86]   Hereinafter referred to as "DOJ Factors." The text of the Justice Department's guidance document is set forth in full in Appendix C to this Guide.

[87]   In addition, it is our understanding that many EPA and state prosecutors rely on this guidance in making prosecutorial decisions.

These factors are not intended to constitute a definitive recipe or checklist of requirements. They are simply illustrations of some of the types of information that are relevant to the Department's exercise of its prosecutorial discretion.[88/]

6.2.1   Voluntary Disclosure

Department of Justice attorneys will consider whether the person made a *voluntary, timely* and *complete* disclosure of the matter under investigation. A disclosure is considered to be voluntary only if it is not required by law, regulation or permit.[89/] Criminal action is less likely if the disclosure is made promptly after discovery of the noncompliance and before a law enforcement or regulatory authority has already obtained knowledge regarding the noncompliance. The Department will consider both the quantity and the quality of the disclosure and the extent to which the disclosure aids the government's investigatory process.[90/]

[88/]   DOJ Factors at 2.

[89/]   See, *e.g.,* Toxic Substances Control Act, 15 U.S.C. § 2607(e); Federal Water Pollution Control Act, 33 U.S.C. § 1321(b)(3)-(5), as amended by the Oil Pollution Act of 1990, 33 U.S.C. § 2701-61; Comprehensive Environmental Response, Compensation, and Liability Act, 42 U.S.C. § 9603(a); Emergency Planning and Community Right-to-Know Act, 42 U.S.C. § 11004.

[90/]   DOJ Factors at 3.

6.2.2   Cooperation

A company's full and prompt cooperation with the prosecuting entity is essential, whether in the context of a voluntary disclosure or after the government has independently learned of a violation. The Department will consider the violator's willingness to make all relevant information available to the government investigators and prosecutors, including the results of any internal or external investigation and the names of all potential witnesses. Consideration will be given to the extent and the quality of the violator's assistance.[91]

6.2.3   Preventive Measures and Compliance Programs

The Department of Justice attorney will consider the existence and scope of any "regularized, intensive, and comprehensive" environmental compliance program.[92] Particular consideration will be given to whether the compliance program includes sufficient measures to identify and prevent future noncompliance, and whether the program was adopted in good faith in a timely manner.

---

[91]   *Id.* at 3-4.

[92]   *Id.* at 4-5.

The federal prosecutor will look at the following factors in evaluating any environmental compliance program:

- whether there was a strong institutional policy to comply with all environmental requirements

- whether safeguards beyond what is required by law were developed and implemented to prevent noncompliance

- whether there existed regular procedures, such as internal or external audits, to evaluate, detect, prevent and remedy circumstances such as those that led to the noncompliance

- whether procedures existed to ensure the integrity of any audit

- whether the audit evaluated all sources of pollution, including the possibility of cross-media transfers of pollutants

- whether the auditor's recommendations were implemented in a timely fashion

- whether adequate resources were committed to the auditing program and to implementing the recommendations

- whether environmental compliance was a standard by which employee and corporate departmental performance was judged.[93]

---

[93]   *Id.*

6.2.4   Pervasiveness of Noncompliance

Pervasive noncompliance will weigh in favor of bringing criminal charges against a company. In determining the pervasiveness of noncompliance, the Justice Department attorney will consider the number and level of employees participating in the unlawful activities, and the obviousness, seriousness, duration, history, and frequency of noncompliance.[94]

6.2.5   Internal Disciplinary Action

The Department guidance states that effective internal disciplinary action is "crucial" to any compliance program. The Justice Department attorney will consider whether there was an effective system of discipline for employees who violated company environmental compliance policies and whether the disciplinary system established an awareness in other employees that unlawful conduct will not be condoned.[95]

---

[94]   *Id.* at 5.

[95]   *Id.*

6.2.6   Subsequent Compliance Efforts

The prosecutor will consider the promptness and completeness of any efforts to remedy any ongoing noncompliance. Considerable weight will be given to good-faith efforts to reach compliance agreements with federal and/or state authorities.[96]

6.3   OTHER FACTORS RELEVANT TO THE EXERCISE OF PROSECUTORIAL DISCRETION

6.3.1   Criminal Actions Against Companies

Contrary to popular belief, most prosecutions for environmental crimes are not of the small midnight dumpers, but are of legitimate established corporations and senior corporate officials. Although in the early years of environmental prosecutions the bulk of criminal sentences and jail terms were levied against small companies, that appears to be changing. A survey of defendants in recent criminal prosecutions reveals a number of Fortune 500 and other prominent companies. Prosecutors may be more inclined to bring criminal charges against such companies because of their visibility and the resulting deterrent effect of a conviction.

---

[96]   *Id.* at 5-6.

Factors that may come into play in a prosecutor's decision whether to bring criminal charges under the environmental statutes include:

- the potential environmental harm or endangerment caused by the noncompliance;

- the company's economic gain resulting from the noncompliance;

- the existence of a pattern of violations by the company;

- a threat to the integrity of the regulatory program's system of recordkeeping and reporting;

- the corporation's attitude concerning environmental compliance; and

- the deterrent effect of a prosecution.[97]

Prosecutors are more likely to bring criminal charges when they believe they have a good "jury case." An example of such a case would be one in which there is evidence of clear intent to violate the environmental laws or a blatant disregard for the laws, and there is environmental damage or harm to humans

---

[97]   In addition, in recent years, most environmental criminal prosecutions have resulted from four types of events: (1) an accident or spill, (2) chronic civil noncompliance, (3) a report by a disgruntled employee or whistle-blower, or (4) an investigator who was angered by a rude or arrogant employee or manager during an inspection. "Environmental Audits May Improve Compliance, But Beware of Disclosure, Attorneys Caution," 22 Environment Reporter (BNA) 1195 (Aug. 30, 1991). It is therefore important to prevent these types of situations whenever possible.

caused by the violation. Cases where there is no clear evidence of intent or ones that involve only recordkeeping violations are less likely to be enforced criminally.

6.3.2　　　Criminal Actions Against Individuals

In deciding whether to bring a criminal action against a particular corporate official, Federal and state prosecutors will consider a number of factors including the following:

- Was the official in a position to have known about the noncompliance or should he or she have known about it?

- Was the official in a position to do something about the noncompliance?

- Did the official consciously avoid or disregard doing something about the noncompliance?

- Is there a connection (a "factual nexus") between the noncompliance and the conduct of the official?

It is Department of Justice policy to pursue criminal enforcement of individuals only when the individual had actual knowledge of the criminal act. There need not, however, be any active participation in the criminal act -- knowing acquiescence in the corporate noncompliance is enough to warrant a criminal prosecution. The responsible corporate officer doctrine is discussed in Chapter 2.

6.4   STEPS TO REDUCE THE LIKELIHOOD OF BEING A TARGET OF A CRIMINAL ENFORCEMENT ACTION

As the Department of Justice guidance makes clear, superficial efforts to demonstrate environmental goodwill are not enough to avert a prosecution should a violation occur. An internal environmental audit program without an effective program for implementing the recommendations of the audit, for example, could do more harm than good. Rather than dissuading the government from pressing charges, an audit could be a "smoking gun" that aids a prosecutor's case and demonstrates the corporate officers' knowledge of violations.

The following factors are essential to developing a corporate environmental compliance program that will reduce the likelihood that your company will be the target of a criminal action:

- The company should have a policy to promptly disclose to appropriate regulatory authorities any noncompliance discovered in the course of an internal audit or otherwise.[98]

---

[98] It usually will not be in a company's interests to disclose a violation without (continued...)

- There should be a clear system for the prompt notification of supervisors when an employee discovers a possible violation. Such notification should be strongly encouraged by management.

- The company should have a policy to cooperate fully with regulators and prosecutors.

- The company should have a comprehensive environmental compliance program which includes internal or external audits and procedures for implementing the audit recommendations. Response to audit results should be immediate, and should be designed to go beyond compliance.

- There should be a strong corporate commitment to spend money to ensure environmental compliance, for example to establish employee training programs, and to allow the appropriate use of outside consultants.

- The company should develop a strong corporate policy for environmental compliance, a "corporate culture" of environmental concern, and should take steps to make that policy known both inside and outside of the company. This would include establishing a policy of swift and severe discipline for employees who knowingly violate the company's compliance policy or otherwise cause compliance concerns.

- The company should establish good relationships with state and Federal regulatory agencies and should communicate openly with such regulators and with the public about environmental issues. The company should strive to achieve a reputation as a "good environmental citizen."

- The company should establish comprehensive procedures for inspections by regulatory agencies, which specify who is to accompany inspectors and how employees should respond when an inspector is on the premises.

28/(...continued)
first involving inside or outside environmental counsel to negotiate on the company's behalf.

Compliance procedures are an essential part of any environmental management policy; however, organizations must also be prepared to respond to a government investigation. Often these investigations begin without much warning and corporate counsel is called upon to respond immediately. Accordingly, an understanding of the process of government investigations and the appropriate response is critical.

CHAPTER 7

RESPONDING APPROPRIATELY TO CRIMINAL INVESTIGATIONS

7.1   GOVERNMENT USE OF SEARCH WARRANTS

There are many devices available to a prosecutor or investigator when conducting a criminal investigation. The two primary devices for obtaining documents and physical evidence are the grand jury subpoena and the search warrant. While a grand jury has broad powers to demand production of documents and to bring before it persons with knowledge or information concerning an investigation, the process is formal, time consuming and cumbersome. By contrast, a search warrant affords no notice to the party from whom documents are sought. Thus, use of a search warrant prevents destruction of evidence, and the assertion of legal objections to the search. The surprise (and usually panic) attendant to execution of a warrant by armed law enforcement officers also provides an unparalleled opportunity for the government to obtain statements from unprepared, unrepresented corporate employees.

Given the complex nature of environmental crimes, many prosecutors prefer to use search warrants. A search warrant provides the optimal vehicle for uncovering evidence and interviewing potential witnesses.

In order to obtain a search warrant, the government must demonstrate by sworn evidence (usually an affidavit) presented to a United States magistrate that there is probable cause to believe an offense has been committed and that items related to the offense will be found on the premises to be searched. The warrant must describe the place to be searched and the persons or things to be seized. At the time the warrant is executed, a copy of the warrant itself and of the inventory of items seized will be left with the person in charge of the premises searched. The affidavit in support of the warrant is not left as a matter of routine; indeed, the affidavit is frequently sealed by order of the issuing magistrate.

7.2   LIMITS ON SEARCH WARRANTS

A search warrant may be attacked if it was issued without a showing of probable cause that a crime has been committed and if the materials related to the crime are not located in the areas to be searched. Also, a warrant may be attacked if it is ambiguous, vague or uncertain. Seizures made pursuant to a search warrant can be challenged as resulting from an improper warrant or from an overbroad search (*e.g.* beyond the scope of the warrant). Items may be seized only if they are (1) evidence of, (2) fruits of, (3) were used in, or (4) aided in commission of a crime, or are otherwise criminally possessed.

7.3 RECEIPT OF THE WARRANT/MONITORING THE INVESTIGATION

Every facility should have an official charged with coordinating the company's response to search warrants. If necessitated by the size of the facility, records custodians familiar with the location and content of files, etc., for sub-units of the facility should be identified and available to the central coordinator. When Government agents arrive with a search warrant, the designated official should contact the company's attorney immediately.

The following issues should be considered by a company and its attorney when a search warrant is served:

- Is it possible/appropriate to send home all but key employees? Keep in mind that anyone left on premises during execution of the warrant may create problems by (a) making ill-advised, uninformed statements to the government agents while unrepresented and feeling vulnerable; (b) saying or doing something that suggests consent to a broader search than that authorized by the warrant; (c) appearing less than cooperative or even obstructive of the search; and/or (d) fueling the rumor mill, contributing to public misperceptions about the nature, scope or source of the investigation.

- Should outside legal counsel with experience in the myriad of issues which inevitably arise during the search be contacted?

- Can contact be established, directly or through outside legal counsel, with the prosecutor in charge of the investigation? This step may be crucial to favorable resolution of issues that come up in the course of the search. It is also likely to result in the company's obtaining more information about the nature of the investigation than would otherwise result from the search, and it may produce a copy of the search warrant affidavit where production thereof is refused at the search site.

- Is it feasible/reasonable/necessary to get counsel to the site of the search? Frequently counsel is required to rely on open telephone lines and effective non-lawyer coordination at the search site.

At the site, the designated official should do at least the following:

- Get a copy of the warrant and, if possible, the affidavit, and fax them to the company's legal counsel.

- Inquire into and determine the procedures which the agents intend to follow in conducting their search, and communicate same to counsel.

- Attempt to establish with the executing agents a procedure under which all general or logistical inquiries arising during the execution of the warrant are directed to such designated official unless and until counsel arrives at the facility.

- Designate off-limits areas, *e.g.*, where privileged files are maintained, where no responsive materials would be found. While agents may disregard such a designation and search the off-limits area, the action may enhance future legal challenges.

- Identify each executing agent present, by credentials if possible, by name, agency and office location.

- Determine, if possible, whether any related search warrants (for individual corporate officers or for corporate affiliates, for example) have been issued.

Agents should never be left unescorted. Ideally, a corporate employee or attorney should be assigned to monitor each agent on premises. Officials should escort agents at all times and note all activities undertaken, *e.g.*, whether agents confine their search to the areas set forth in the warrant; the conduct, statements and questions posed by the agents; which, if any, employees are interviewed, including comments made in the agent's presence. Agents are not required to accept the presence of an escort when interrogating witnesses. However, when excluded, an escort can stand nearby and, if possible, observe the interrogation, noting the demeanor of the agent, the length of the interview, the passing of documentary or physical evidence, or other relevant conduct.

The warrant should be reviewed by an attorney to ensure that it is specific in its description of the location to be searched, that it describes unambiguously the inspection functions to be performed, and that the on-site official coordinating for the corporation knows what areas are specified and advises the agent-in-charge what areas are beyond the scope of the warrant. Careful review is critical. The company may deny government agents access to areas not specifically set forth in the warrant.

The company's attorney should take every opportunity to ascertain the government's reason for seeking the search warrant, by attempting to secure a copy of the affidavit in support of the search warrant and otherwise. If the agents and/or prosecutor are unwilling to provide a copy of the affidavit on the day of the search, a copy can be requested from the clerk of the U.S. District Court. In some jurisdictions the clerk will not provide a copy until the Government files its return of the warrant (usually within several days of the search).

During and immediately after the search, the company and its counsel should do the following:

- Prevent any employees remaining on premises from attempting to interfere with the search.

- Prevent such employees from volunteering comments to investigators which might be harmful to employees or to the company.

- Prevent employees from making statements which could be construed as granting consent to extend the search beyond the bounds of the warrant.

- Protest any searches or seizures not within the scope of the warrant.

- Compile as detailed a record as possible of the activities of each agent, including an inventory of all items seized. The inventory is in addition to the "receipt" that will be provided by the agents. Where possible, get copies of documents taken. They may be necessary for continuation of business after the search, will be instructive on the evidence in the government's hands, and may preclude the need for filing a motion for return of documents.

- Interview all employees who had any contact with the search to determine: a) what was seized, b) where it was located, c) whether the employee said anything to the investigators, d) whether the employee heard anyone else say anything to the investigators, e) whether the investigators said anything overheard by the employee.

- Compile a written report of what took place during the search giving all available detail. This will assist in assessing possible attacks on the warrant and/or search and in preparation of a defense.

- Request an exit interview and debriefing session with the investigators.

- In the event that the investigator takes samples of wastes or other materials, counsel should demand a receipt describing the sample obtained, a portion of each sample equal in volume or weight to the portion retained by the Government and a description of the tests the Government intends to perform on the samples. If the Government is unwilling to share its samples, counsel should ensure that samples are taken immediately, from the same source(s), by the company.

- Counsel should demand copies of any photographs taken by Government agents, as well as record the area encompassed by each photograph.

Government agents must provide the company with a receipt for any property taken pursuant to the warrant. The receipt and the property or documents should be carefully compared.

Private contractors employed by the government to conduct sampling may or may not be authorized representatives of the government and the company may be able to exclude such contractors from the premises.

The search warrant process can be quite dangerous and can bring unexpected results. For example, where a government agent conducting a search pursuant to a warrant writes down information from a document but does not actually take the document, no "seizure" has occurred. Thus, unless the warrant is defective, an agent can record almost any information from a corporation's records and never be challenged. In the course of a search, extraneous items may be examined and read in order to determine whether they fall within the scope of the warrant. Thus, the issuance of a search warrant may result in a fishing expedition where the government discovers evidence or information neither contemplated by the affidavit supporting the warrant nor covered by the warrant itself. Also, government agents will read and make notes from documents marked as "attorney-client privileged" or as "attorney work product."

The search and seizure process in an environmental case can resemble a blitzkrieg attack. Such a situation can be chaotic and dangerous. A quick corporate response, including detailed monitoring of the search by attorneys, is essential.

CHAPTER 8

THE FEDERAL SENTENCING GUIDELINES
AND ENVIRONMENTAL CRIME PENALTIES

As a result of the Sentencing Reform Act of 1984 and the promulgation of the Federal Sentencing Guidelines[29] those convicted of environmental crimes will be dealt with harshly. The purpose of the Sentencing Guidelines was to create a set of mandatory guidelines which would treat various classes of offenders consistently. A mandatory range of determinate sentences for each level of Federal offense has been established, and a court may depart from the guideline range only if it finds a mitigating or aggravating factor which the Sentencing Commission did not adequately consider. Any such departure must be supported by a statement of reasons.

8.1   SENTENCING GUIDELINES FOR INDIVIDUALS

The Sentencing Commission identified environmental offenses as regulatory offenses that are "particularly important in light of the need for

---

[29]   The Sentencing Guidelines for individuals took effect on November 1, 1987. The organizational guidelines which do not currently cover environmental crimes, were approved by the Sentencing Commission on April 26, 1991 and became effective November 1, 1991. On March 5, 1993 the Advisory Work Group on Environmental Sanctions released a working draft of sentencing guidelines for organizations convicted of Federal environmental crimes. The draft guidelines are set forth in Appendix D to this Guide.

enforcement of the general regulatory scheme."[100]

The Sentencing Guidelines abolished parole for environmental crimes defendants in order "to ensure that the sentence imposed . . . is the sentence the offender will serve."[101] The Guidelines severely restrict the use of probation, an outcome which had been the norm in environmental crime cases. As a result of these two changes, those convicted of environmental crimes are seeing much more jail time. After a manager of a Tennessee electroplating plant was sentenced to 40 months in jail, Barry Hartman, acting Assistant Attorney General, pointed out the most direct effect of such a long sentence: "The days of the businessman writing off environmental violations as simply a cost of doing business are gone."[102]

The amount of jail time an individual will serve depends on a number of factors. The sentence range from which a judge will choose is based on an offense level and a criminal history category. The basic offense level depends on the particular crime, but the specific characteristics of the individual's violation

---

[100] United States Sentencing Commission, *Federal Sentencing Guidelines Manual,* ch.1, pt.A, p.8. (1991).

[101] *See* Starr & Kelly, "Environmental Crimes and the Sentencing Guidelines : The Time Has Come . . . and It Is Hard Time," 20 Envtl. L. Rep. 10096, 10100 (March 1990).

[102] "Tennessee Man Gets 40-Month Sentence for Illegal Waste Disposal at Business," 22 Environment Reporter (BNA) 1025 (Aug. 9, 1991).

will adjust the basic offense level upwards or downwards. A typical case is *United States v. Pozsgai*,[103] in which the owner of a truck repair business was sentenced to 27 months in prison for violating the Clean Water Act by adding topsoil to his property that was classified as a wetland.[104]

Courts have been quite strict in their application of the adjustments, as well. For example, in *United States v. Goldfaden*[105], the court upheld upward enhancements: for continuous discharges (although there was no proof of actual environmental contamination), for discharge without a permit (although there would not have been a violation at all if there was a permit), and for obstruction of justice (perjury). Due to the obstruction of justice, the court also upheld the lower court's denial of a reduction of the offense level for acceptance of responsibility. The strict use of enhancement provisions added 27 months to the minimum and maximum sentences the defendant could receive.

For those who feel prison sentences for first-time environmental offenders are uncalled for, courts already have provided a response. When William Ellen was sentenced to six months in prison for the filling of wetlands, he protested

---

[103]   No. CR-88-00450 (E.D.Pa. July 13, 1989), *affirmed*, 897 F.2d 524 (3d. Cir), *cert. den.*, 111 S. Ct. 48 (1990).

[104]   For cases illustrating jail time for environmental criminal defendants in the wake of the Sentencing Guidelines, see *United States v. Sellers*, 926 F.2d 410 (5th Cir. 1991); *United States v. Wells Metal Finishing, Inc.*, 922 F.2d 54 (1st Cir. 1991).

[105]   959 F.2d 1324 (5th Cir. 1992).

that his crime was not serious enough to warrant jail time under the guidelines. The appeals court was unsympathetic: "[t]hat Ellen believes that an offense of this magnitude is trivial or unimportant ironically exemplifies the need not to foreclose punishment by imprisonment in enforcing laws aimed at environmental protection." [106] The draft recommendations for sanctioning organizations convicted of federal environmental crimes combine harsh penalties with consideration of mitigating factors.

8.2   SENTENCING GUIDELINES FOR ORGANIZATIONS

Corporations convicted of Federal crimes committed in whole or in part after November 1, 1991 are subject to stringent sentencing guidelines: the United States Sentencing Commission's Sentencing Guidelines for Organizational Defendants ("Guidelines" or "U.S.S.G."). The Guidelines affect the way in which a court determines a corporation's sentence as well as the severity of the corporation's punishment. In addition to imposing a fine, a court may require a corporation to make restitution to a victim, serve probation, disgorge profits from its criminal activity and completely divest its assets.

The Guidelines, however, do not necessarily spell doom for a convicted

---

[106]   *United States v. Ellen*, 961 F.2d 462, 468 (4th Cir.) *cert. den.*, 113 S. Ct. 217 (1992).

corporation. In addition to meting out punishment for offenses committed, the Guidelines encourage corporations to institute and maintain internal mechanisms for preventing, detecting and reporting criminal conduct. Consequently, the Guidelines allow for mitigation of a sentence based upon the corporation's adoption of an effective compliance program or demonstration of other positive behavior.

8.2.1 Fines

The Guidelines fine provisions for sentencing organizations do not currently apply to environmental crimes. Draft recommendations for sentencing organizations convicted of environmental crimes have been released. These draft recommendations propose a formula for establishing a base fine that can be increased by aggravating factors. The proposed aggravating factors include:

- management involvement
- threat to the environment
- knowing violations of the law
- criminal compliance history
- civil compliance history
- concealment of a violation
- violation of an order

- ● absence of a compliance program or other organized effort

Factors proposed for consideration that would reduce the base fine include:

- ● commitment to environmental compliance

- ● cooperation and self-reporting

- ● lack of intent to violate the law

- ● remedial assistance

The draft recommendations have not been adopted and do not currently apply to environmental crimes.

Until Guideline provisions for environmental crime fines are adopted, the Guidelines state that such fines are to be "based on the general statutory provisions governing sentencing." U.S.S.G. § 8C2.10, background note. Further, environmental damage is a factor that is considered in fining organizations convicted of other crimes. One of the Guidelines' policy statements provides: "[i]f the offense presented a threat to the environment, an upward departure [from the base fine level] may be warranted."[107] Given these factors, and the *Exxon* judge's refusal of a proposed fine because the Guidelines would have imposed a higher one, corporations must not ignore any aspect of the Guidelines.

---

[107] U.S.S.G. § 8C4.4.

8.2.2 Probation and Other Non-Monetary Penalties

The Guidelines require that probation for a term not to exceed five years be imposed on a corporation if any of the following conditions exist:

- it is necessary to ensure restitution or completion of community service

- a monetary penalty has not been paid in full

- the corporation has at least 50 employees but no effective compliance program

- the corporation was convicted of a similar offense within five years prior to sentencing

- a high-level employee participated in the offense and was convicted of similar misconduct within five years prior to sentencing

- it is necessary to ensure that sufficient changes are made to minimize the chance of future criminal conduct

- it is necessary to reflect the seriousness of the offense, promote respect for the law, provide just punishment for the offense, afford adequate deterrence, or protect the public from further crimes.

The nature of a probationary sentence may vary. While implementation of a compliance program is mandatory, a court has the discretion, as a term of probation, to order, for example, environmental cleanup, creation of a trust fund, removal of a director, or community service. Probation can force a corporation to change its behavior dramatically.

The Guidelines also provide for an order requiring a corporation to make restitution to all victims of the offense and to remedy any harm caused by it.

Many first-time offending corporations should be able to avoid court-imposed probation by fulfilling all of the requirements listed above. The most significant requirement, and the most difficult to show, however, will be "an effective program to prevent and detect violations of law." A corporation must have a well thought out compliance program if it intends to argue that despite its instant transgression, it does indeed have an effective system to prevent violations.

APPENDICES

APPENDICES

PAGE

APPENDIX A: U.S. JUSTICE DEPARTMENT PROCEDURES
BETWEEN U.S. ATTORNEYS' OFFICES AND
DOJ HEADQUARTERS: Recent Amendments
to Chapter 11 Of Title 5 Of The
United States Attorneys' Manual
(Jan. 13, 1993) 101

APPENDIX B: NEW JERSEY VOLUNTARY ENVIRONMENTAL
AUDIT/COMPLIANCE GUIDELINES 114

APPENDIX C: FACTORS IN DECISIONS ON CRIMINAL
PROSECUTIONS FOR ENVIRONMENTAL
VIOLATIONS IN THE CONTEXT OF
SIGNIFICANT VOLUNTARY COMPLIANCE OR
DISCLOSURE EFFORTS BY THE VIOLATOR 121

APPENDIX D: WORKING DRAFT RECOMMENDATIONS BY
THE ADVISORY WORKING GROUP ON
ENVIRONMENTAL SANCTIONS TO THE
UNITED STATES SENTENCING COMMISSION ... 132

APPENDIX A

U.S. JUSTICE DEPARTMENT PROCEDURES BETWEEN
U.S. ATTORNEYS' OFFICES AND DOJ HEADQUARTERS

Recent Amendments To Chapter 11 Of Title 5
Of The United States Attorneys' Manual

January 13, 1993

APPENDIX A

**U.S. JUSTICE DEPARTMENT PROCEDURES BETWEEN
U.S. ATTORNEYS' OFFICES AND DOJ HEADQUARTERS:**
Recent Amendments To Chapter 11 Of Title 5
Of The United States Attorneys' Manual
(Jan. 13, 1993)

Subject: Procedures for the Handling of Environmental Criminal Cases By
United States Attorney's Offices and the Environment and Natural
Resources Division of the United States Department of Justice

5-11.110   General Responsibilities

A. Primary responsibility for cases arising under the statutes identified in
USAM 5-11.101 may rest with the U.S. Attorney's Office, with the
Environmental Crimes Section, or with both on a shared basis. That
responsibility will be determined on a case-by-case basis. Experience has
demonstrated that very satisfactory results may be obtained from a cooperative,
joint effort, combining the U.S. Attorney's Office's familiarity with local practices
and procedures and the Environmental Crimes Section's subject matter expertise
and experience gained in conducting grand jury proceedings and trials in similar
cases.

B. There are no precise rules for determining how responsibility for a
criminal environmental case is to be divided between the U.S. Attorney's Office
and the Environmental Crimes Section. The decision for a given case will be
made ultimately by the Assistant Attorney General of the Environment and
Natural Resources Division in consultation with the U.S. Attorney.
Investigations/cases are divided into three categories:

1. Environmental Crimes Section ("ECS") cases;

2. USAO cases; and

3. joint cases.

- ECS cases will be handled by the ECS attorney assigned, while the USAO will designate a liaison AUSA to assist with local rules and protocols and final review of the indictment, plea or other disposition.

- USAO cases will be handled by a designated AUSA, while ECS will designate an ECS attorney for consultation and for final review of the indictment, plea or other disposition.

- Joint cases will be handled by a designated AUSA and a designated ECS attorney; all scheduling and planning will be done jointly by the attorneys.

C. Both the Division and the Environmental Crimes Subcommittee of the Attorney General's Advisory Committee acknowledge that optimum results in environmental cases historically have occurred in instances when cases are investigated and prosecuted as joint cases, and that such cases generally make the most efficient and effective use of the respective resources of the Division and USAOs. Accordingly, these Guidelines are intended not to discourage, but to encourage the formation of relationships that will lead to the development of working partnerships between AUSAs and ECS attorneys and the free and open discussion of all matters, with the likelihood that they will be handled jointly to the extent of available resources.

D. In cases handled entirely by the U.S. Attorneys, in which the Environmental Crimes Section takes no direct role in the litigation, Section resources are available to provide support for the efforts of the U.S. Attorneys. For example, Section attorneys may do legal research, prepare draft papers, and provide advice on policy questions and on related cases in other districts. In cases handled primarily by the Environmental Crimes Section, the United States Attorney's Offices shall cooperate by assisting Section attorneys in scheduling sufficient grand jury time to allow investigations to proceed in timely fashion.

E. It is recognized that there will be some USAO investigations/cases which will necessarily be more significant in scope, complexity or issues and thus subject to a need for greater review and control. The Division will identify those issues of importance which will require such scrutiny. Those cases which are currently subject to such review and control include:

1. Resource Conservation and Recovery Act violations, where a defense has been raised, or is reasonably likely to be raised, that an alleged hazardous waste is not "solid waste" under applicable statutes and regulations.

2. Wetlands violations;

3. Charges under the Clean Air Act Amendments except for asbestos cases;

4. Knowing endangerment charges;

5. Charges based on negligence (except where such charges are part of a charge reduction as a result of a plea agreement);

6. Violations based upon a strict liability theory (except where such charges are part of a charge reduction as a result of a plea agreement);

7. Charges based upon the "responsible corporate officer doctrine";

8. Federal facilities;

9. Matters involving evidence to be presented by the Government derived in whole or in part from self-auditing by regulated entities or otherwise implicating the July 1, 1991 Policy on Audits and Voluntary Disclosure; and

10. Any matter of national interest, for example, an initial prosection under a particular statute or regulation, or a prosecution involving application of a regulation the validity of which is significantly in doubt.[108]

---

[108] The term "national interest" is not intended to be a catch-all phrase to obviate these Guidelines. For any case designated as a priority case on the ground that it involves national interest, ECS will identify in writing to the USAO the specific factors upon which such a designation is based.

Whenever there is to be a modification of these categories (hereinafter, "priority categories"), the Environmental Crimes Subcommittee of the Attorney General's Advisory Committee will be consulted by the Environment and Natural Resources Division. The Subcommittee will assist in the identification of issues that require greater scrutiny on the part of the Division. In any event, there will be an annual review of the aforementioned priorities at the subcommittee meeting which immediately follows each U.S. Attorney's Conference.

5-11.200 ORGANIZATION

5-11.210 General

The Section is administered by a Chief and an Assistant Chief. General information relating to the Section or to matters for which it is responsible may be obtained by calling the Chief at (202) 272-9877. Information on a specific case should be requested from the staff attorney assigned to that case. When the staff attorney's name is unknown, his or her name and telephone number can be obtained by calling (202) 272-9877. (Note that a quicker response to an inquiry may be forthcoming if the requestor can cite a Departmental file number, e.g., 198-13-12, which generally appears in the upper left hand corner of correspondence originating from the Department.)

5-11.300 HANDLING OF CRIMINAL ENVIRONMENTAL CASES, GENERALLY

5-11.301 Case Development [unchanged]

5-11.302 Environmental Case Initiation

A. The ordinary procedure for initiation of criminal cases arising under the statutes identified in USAM 5-11.101, supra, and originating from EPA is by simultaneous referral to the Assistant Attorney General, Environment and Natural Resources Division and to the U.S. Attorney in the district with jurisdiction over the matter. Referral packages generally contain investigative reports and various exhibits which may aid in the understanding of the referral. However, in many instances, it may be necessary to complete the development of the cases through the use of the grand jury.

B. Some cases, though, are initiated without or prior to a formal referral, for example, when investigators call upon the U.S. Attorney's Offices to secure search warrants or when exigent circumstances require early resort to grand jury proceedings. The U.S. Attorney's Office shall advise the Environmental Crimes Section of all such situations by submitting a case initiation report.

C. The USAOs and ECS will each promptly advise the other of the initiation of any investigation, and will share information in a timely fashion as facts are developed.

D. Submission of a Case Initiation Report ("CIR"). Within two weeks of the initiation of a case by a USAO, it will submit a CIR to the Chief of ECS. Similarly, within two weeks of the initiation of a case by ECS, it will submit a CIR to the AUSA having supervisory authority for environmental prosecutions at the appropriate USAO. The CIR will include: (i) a summary of the investigation, including a statement of the available evidence to date, identification of subjects and targets, and the object and purpose of the investigation; (ii) an identification of the responsible investigative agency and case agent; (iii) a clear identification of the statute and regulations suspected to have been violated; and (iv) a statement of the USAO's or ECS's view as to whether or not the case falls into one of the priority categories, supra. An investigation will be deemed initiated at the earliest of the following dates: (i) the date it is opened as a matter in the USAO Promis, Eagle or other internal docketing system or the Division's internal docketing system (LDTS); (ii) the date an AUSA or ECS attorney provides a prosecutive opinion to the investigating agency or agent; or (iii) the date the USAO or ECS attorney issues the first grand jury subpoena. When a case is initiated by ECS, the U.S. Attorney will designate a liaison AUSA immediately upon receipt of the CIR from ECS and notify ECS of that designation.

E. ECS will utilize a centralized internal docketing system which will document the receipt of the CIR from the USAO.

5-11.303   Authority to Prosecute; Retention of Authority; Contact with Defense Counsel; Requests for Assistance

A. Within twenty-one (21) days of the receipt of the CIR from a USAO, ECS will inform the USA whether the case falls within one of the priority categories, supra. A declaration that a case is a priority should be made in writing in order to clearly state the basis for that decision; such cases will be denominated as "PRIORITY CASES." For any investigation determined by ECS not to be a PRIORITY CASE, the USAO will promptly provide an updated CIR immediately to the Chief of ECS if and when an issue arises in the investigation that might arguably cause it to fall into one of the priority categories.

   B. In all USAO cases designated as "PRIORITY CASES", the USAO will submit all indictments, pleas (including global settlements) or other proposed dispositions to ECS for approval so that they are received at least 10 business days before the anticipated action. With respect to each submission, the USAO shall submit two copies -- one to the attention of the ECS attorney assigned to the case, and the second to the attention of the Chief of ECS, or in his or her absence, the Acting Chief. ECS will complete its review within 5 business days following receipt of the submission, unless it determines that additional information is essential to that review, which determination it will communicate to the USAO by telephone and confirm in writing. Priority indictments or plea proposals will be submitted for review along with a brief prosecution memorandum. For those cases designed as "PRIORITY CASES", a veto of the United States Attorney's recommendation must be based upon specific reasons set forth in writing.

   C. Non Priority Cases do not require approval. In all such cases, the USAO will promptly provide copies of indictments, informations, dispositions, and other significant pleadings to ECS, and is encouraged to consult with ECS.

   D. Contact with defense counsel on cases being handled jointly by USAO and ECS will also include a representative of ECS and the particular USAO. In all USAO cases, all defense counsel contact should be referred in the first instance directly to the USAO. In all ECS cases, all defense counsel contact should be referred in the first instance directly to ECS. Furthermore, in all cases, whether USAO, ECS or joint, both the U.S. Attorney and the Assistant Attorney General of the Environment and Natural Resources Division ("AAG") retain discretion to meet with defense counsel, subject only to the following: if the AAG chooses to meet with defense counsel in a USAO or joint case, he or she will invite the U.S. Attorney to attend the meeting either in person or through a representative, and will schedule the meeting to facilitate that attendance; similarly, if the U.S. Attorney chooses to meet with defense counsel in an ECS or joint case, he or she will invite the AAG to attend the meeting either in person or through a representative, and will schedule the meeting to facilitate that attendance. Any such meeting, whether scheduled by the U.S. Attorney or the AAG will be held at a location to be mutually agreed upon by the U.S. Attorney and the AAG.

E. To the extent that either ECS or a USAO is in need of additional legal support for a particular case or matter, each will seek to obtain it from the other. Only in the event that no AUSA or ECS attorney is available will either resort to other resources, such as agency counsel.

5-11.304   Information Needed to be Furnished to the Environmental Crimes Section by the U.S. Attorney's Office [modified by revisions to other sections]

5-11.305   Parallel Proceedings [unchanged]

5-11.306   Cases Arising by Other Than Agency Referral

U.S. Attorneys retain their authority to prosecute cases under statutes listed in USAM-5.101, supra, which are not developed or referred to them from a federal agency. The U.S. Attorney shall notify the Assistant Attorney General of the Environment and Natural Resources Division of the initiation of any such prosecution under the statutes <u>identified in USAM 5-11.101</u>, supra, to enable the Environment and Natural Resources Division to perform its oversight responsibilities for prosecution under those statutes as set forth herein.

5-11.307   Other Cases Involving Environmental Violations

Whenever, in the context of a case not otherwise within the jurisdiction of the Environment and Natural Resources division, a U.S. Attorney becomes aware of the information which indicates that such case may include violations of any statute identified in USAM 5-11.101, supra, the U.S. Attorney shall advise the Assistant Attorney General of the Environment and Natural Resources Division of that possibility. Upon request of the Assistant Attorney General, the U.S. Attorney shall forward to the Assistant Attorney General copies of relevant material, including grand jury transcripts.

5-11.308   Coordination with State Programs [unchanged]

5-11.310   <u>Conduct of Prosecution</u>

5-11.311   Individual and Corporate Defendants [unchanged]

5-11.312   Attorneys Who May Represent the United States

A. All criminal environmental cases must be handled by attorneys who are either employed by the Department of Justice (including the U.S. Attorney's Offices) or are authorized by the Department to represent the United States. When circumstances require the use of agency attorneys in either a grand jury investigation or the actual litigation of any case involving violations of statutes identified in USAM 5-11.101, supra, prior notification shall be given to the Assistant Attorney General of the Environment and Natural Resources Division. In any case in which the Environment and Natural Resources Division has subject matter jurisdiction, authority for agency attorneys to participate in grand jury investigations or litigation shall be obtained prior to such participation from the Assistant Attorney General of the Environment and Natural Resources Division through the Chief of the Environmental Crimes Section. Any letter of appointment of an agency attorney as a Special Assistant United States Attorney shall be processed through the Environment and Natural Resources Division.

B. Any appointment of any agency attorney to a special status shall specify (1) the scope of the attorney's appointment in terms of subject matter and duration and (2) that the activities of the attorney under the appointment shall be subject to the direction of the U.S. Attorney and/or the Assistant Attorney General of the Environment and Natural Resources Division.

5-11.313   Search Warrants [unchanged]

5-11.314   Grand Jury Subpoenas for Documents

When grand jury subpoenas for documents are being prepared in cases arising under the statutes identified in USAM 5-11.101, U.S. Attorney's Offices are encouraged to contact the Environmental Crimes Section. The experience of Section attorneys with such subpoenas in other cases may be of assistance to the U.S. Attorney's Offices. Copies of grand jury subpoenas for documents shall be furnished to the Environmental Crimes Section in any such cases.

5-11.315   Witness Immunities [unchanged]

5-11.320   **Dispositions**

5-11-321   **Declinations**

A. The U.S. Attorney may decline to prosecute any case arising under the statutes identified in USAM 5-11.101, supra, which is being handled entirely by his/her office, by notifying the Assistant Attorney General of the Environment and Natural Resources Division of his/her decision with an explanation of the reasons for the decision and an explanation of the referring agency's position regarding declination. Informal discussion of such situations between the U.S. Attorney's Office and the Environmental Crimes Section prior to a final decision by the former often facilitates coordination between the two offices.

B. The Assistant Attorney General may choose to prosecute any case declined by a U.S. Attorney, with attorneys of the Environmental Crimes Section conducting such prosecution. The Assistant Attorney General may request from the U.S. Attorney whatever additional information is deemed necessary in order to decide whether to proceed with the prosecution of a referral declined by a U.S. Attorney.

C. The procedures described in the preceding two paragraphs above also shall apply in any case in which a grand jury declines to return a true bill of indictment, if the U.S. Attorney is of the opinion that prosecution should not proceed in such case.

5-11.322   **Dismissals**

Indictments, information, or complaints in criminal cases involving violations of the statutes identified in USAM 5-11.101, supra, shall not be dismissed without prior approval of the Assistant Attorney General of the Environment and Natural Resources Division, except when a superseding indictment has been returned or an information or complaint has been filed against the same defendant or when the individual defendant has died. Recommendations to dismiss criminal cases are the responsibility of the U.S. attorney personally and must be signed by him/her. This provision does not apply to situations involving plea agreements which provide for the dismissal of certain counts of an indictment or information coupled with pleas of guilty to other counts.

5-11.323   **Plea Negotiations and Agreements; "Global Settlements"; Alternative Sentencing [unchanged]**

5-11.324   **Sentencing Memorandum [unchanged]**

5-11.330   <u>**Coordination With the Environmental Crimes Section**</u>

5-11.331   **Case Status**

A. In all USAO cases, the AUSA handling the case is encouraged to submit copies of indictments, information, motion papers, memoranda of law, briefs and other significant documents to ECS so that ECS can fulfill its function of serving as document bank and a clearinghouse of information regarding environmental prosecutions. In addition, the following information should be furnished promptly to the Environmental Crimes Section with regard to all cases:

1. Date the indictment (or no bill) is returned or the information or complaint is filed;

2. Date of arraignment and kind of plea;

3. Date of trial;

4. Verdict;

5. Change of plea of plea agreement;

6. Date of sentencing and terms of sentence;

7. A copy of any search warrant, including its supporting affidavit(s);

8. Copies of such papers filed and correspondence exchanged as are requested by the Environmental Crimes Section attorney assigned to the case.

B. Significant developments should be reported immediately by telephone to the Chief, Environmental Crimes Section, in any case in which the Section requests such reports.

5-11.332   Copies of Documents

The copies of documents required to be furnished to the Environmental Crimes Section under various provisions herein relating to environmental crimes serve at least two important functions. First, they allow the Environmental Crimes Section to function in both an advisory capacity and as a clearing house for ideas which otherwise would not be shared among U.S. Attorney's Offices. Second, they aid the Environmental Crimes Section in performing its monitoring function to avoid the government's taking inconsistent positions on related matters.

5-11.340   <u>Appeals</u>

5-11.341   Handling of Appeals

All appeals in criminal cases arising under the statutes identified in USAM 5-11.101, <u>supra</u>, shall be handled as provided for in USAM 5-8.310 and Title 2, except that, upon the request of the U.S. Attorney and the approval of Assistant Attorney General, Environment and Natural Resources Division, the United States Attorney's Office may take primary responsibility for the handling of an appeal. Any such request should be initiated through the Chief, Environmental Crimes Section. In any case handled by a United States Attorney's Office copies of all briefs shall be furnished to the Environmental Crimes Section and the Appellate Section of the Environment and Natural Resources Division. Copies of any brief of behalf of the government and of any opposing brief(s) shall be forwarded to those Sections in sufficient time to allow review and comment by them prior to any further government briefing.

5-11.342   Notice of Appeals

A. The U.S. Attorney shall immediately notify the Chief of the Environmental Crimes Section of any notice of appeal by a defendant in any case arising under any statute identified in USAM 5-11.101, <u>supra</u>.

B. In any such case in which the U.S. Attorney believes that appeal by the United States is warranted, he/she shall make his/her recommendation to the Chief of the Environmental Crimes Section.

C. For purposes of subparagraphs A and B above, notification and recommendations may be made by telephone in expedited appeal situations.

5-11.343   Record on Appeal

Whenever an appeal is taken in a case arising under any statute identified in USAM 5-11.101, <u>supra</u>, for which the U.S. Attorney has taken primary trial level responsibility, and that appeal is to be handled by the Environment and Natural Resources Division, the U.S. Attorney is responsible for assembling and transmitting to the Environment and Natural Resources Division those items which constitute the record of the case of the trial court level.

APPENDIX B

NEW JERSEY

VOLUNTARY ENVIRONMENTAL AUDIT/COMPLIANCE GUIDELINES

An Initiative of the New Jersey Environmental Prosecutor's
Office Developed in Cooperation with the Divisions of
Criminal Justice and Law, the County Prosecutors'
Association and the Department of Environmental
Protection and Energy

May 15, 1992

Robert J. Del Tufo
Attorney General of New Jersey

Steven J. Madonna, New Jersey
State Environmental Prosecutor

APPENDIX B

NEW JERSEY

VOLUNTARY ENVIRONMENTAL AUDIT/COMPLIANCE GUIDELINES

FACTORS IN THE EXERCISE OF DISCRETION IN DECISIONS ON CRIMINAL PROSECUTIONS FOR ENVIRONMENTAL VIOLATIONS IN THE CONTEXT OF EFFECTIVELY OPERATING VOLUNTARY COMPLIANCE/AUDIT PROGRAMS

I.   Introduction

In order to encourage the adoption and use of voluntary environmental compliance and audit programs by New Jersey business and industry, the New Jersey Attorney General, the State Environmental Prosecutor, the Director of the Division Criminal Justice, and the County Prosecutors have determined that the implementation and operation of such programs shall be viewed as mitigating factors in the exercise of criminal environmental enforcement discretion. This document is intended to describe the factors considered relevant in deciding whether, how, when and against whom to bring a criminal prosecution for a violation of an environmental statute. It is designed to give prosecutors direction concerning the exercise of prosecutorial discretion in environmental criminal cases. It is also intended to give New Jersey business and industry a sense of what to expect from the decision making process in the exercise of prosecutorial discretion in criminal matters when a compliance/audit program has been implemented.

This guidance and the factors contained herein provide a framework for the determination of whether a particular case presents the type of circumstances in which leniency would be appropriate.

II.   Factors to be Considered

Where the law and evidence would otherwise be sufficient for criminal prosecution, the prosecutor should consider the factors contained herein, to the extent they are applicable, along with any other relevant factors, in determining whether to initiate a criminal prosecution, how to shape the charges, the timing of the prosecution, and the identity of the proposed defendants. It must be emphasized that these are examples of the types of factors which could be relevant. They do not constitute a definitive or exhaustive checklist of requirements. They merely illustrate some of the types of information which from time to time may be relevant to the exercise of criminal prosecutorial discretion.

No single factor will be dispositive in any given case. All relevant factors are considered and given the weight deemed appropriate in the circumstances of the particular case.

A. Existence and Scope of Environmental Compliance/Audit Program

The prosecutor should first consider the existence and scope of any environmental compliance/audit program. The program should be in writing and should address each of the environmental media potentially impacted by the company operations.

B. Maintenance, Inspection and Operation Features

The prosecutor should consider the extent to which the program details written procedures requiring the inventorying, inspection, and evaluation of all facilities, equipment, operations, practices, and procedures as to all media; to discover non-compliance; to assess the effectiveness of operation and maintenance procedures; to evaluate the suitability of existing processes and designs; to review and evaluate the effectiveness of employee training and education, employee compliance with policies and procedures, and management, supervision and discipline; to promote pollution prevention; and to maximize reuse and recycling.

C. Adopted and Promoted By Management

The prosecutor should consider the extent to which the preparation, implementation, and operation of the program has been adopted and promoted by the highest levels of the company management and published, disseminated, and enforced as the institutionalized policy of the company.

D. Adequacy of Formal Employee Training

The prosecutor should consider the extent to which the operation of the program has been the subject of formal training of company employees, including training of employees in implementation and adherence procedures, together with regular refresher and update training.

E. Adequacy of Funding, Personnel and Resources

The prosecutor should consider the extent to which funding, personnel, and resources have been made available to insure the effective design, preparation, implementation, and operation of the compliance/audit program.

F. Involvement of Qualified Independent Professionals

The prosecutor should consider the extent of the involvement of qualified professionals, whether in-house or independent, in the design, preparation, implementation, and operation of the compliance/audit program.

G. Existence of Periodic Audit Requirements

The prosecutor should consider the extent to which the program requires the periodic environmental auditing of all facilities, equipment, operations, procedures, and employee practices of the business entity by trained and qualified staff assigned on a facility-wide basis. The prosecutor should also consider the extent to which the audit report enumerates violations occurring during the period, explains the causes, identifies the situations requiring correction, and recommends corrective or other remedial action. The prosecutor should be especially sensitive to the extent that the report recommendations include, as appropriate, acquisition of new equipment, repair or maintenance of equipment, change in operations, practices or procedures, and disciplinary action against employees and any other measures to prevent recurrence. He should also review the audit procedures and safeguards to insure the reasonable integrity of the audit process.

H. Existence of Policy and Practice Regarding Correction, Modification or Remediation

The prosecutor should consider the extent to which the policy and practices of the company provide for the timely and appropriate correction of any procedures or practices; repair, maintenance or replacement of any equipment; modification or elimination of any processes; cleanup, disposal or other remediation; all as may be required in response to audit reports. Of critical importance is the promptness and completeness of any action taken to remove the source of the non-compliance and to lessen the environmental harm resulting from the non-compliance.

I. Existence of Employee Disciplinary Policy and Practice

The prosecutor should consider the extent to which the policy and practices of the company provide for reasonable but effective disciplinary measures in the case of employees failing to follow program procedures. Did the system establish an awareness in other employees that improper/unlawful conduct would not be condoned?

J. Existence of Employee Recognition and Reward Policy and Practice

The prosecutor should consider the extent to which the policy and practices of the company recognize, reward, and foster employee compliance and vigilance, and their involvement in the reporting of incidents of unlawful or criminal environmental practices within the company. Were employees encouraged to use an environmental compliance hotline or other easily available reporting systems? Environmental compliance should be a standard by which employee and company/department performance is judged.

K. Existence and Pervasiveness of Non-Compliance

The prosecutor should consider the existence and pervasiveness of any non-compliance with the environmental laws and regulations and the company's environmental compliance/audit program. The Prosecutor should be especially sensitive when this non-compliance results in environmental degradation. The existence of this condition may indicate systematic or repeated participation in, or condonation of, criminal or unlawful behavior. It may also indicate the lack of a meaningful compliance program. In evaluating this factor, the prosecutor should consider, among other things, the number and level of employees participating in the unlawful activities and the obviousness, seriousness, duration, history, and frequency of noncompliance.

L. Occurrence of Voluntary Disclosure

The prosecutor should consider whether the person/entity made a voluntary, timely and complete disclosure of the matter under investigation. Consideration should be given to whether the person came forward promptly after discovering the noncompliance, and to the quantity and quality of information provided. Particular consideration should be given to whether the disclosure substantially aided the government's investigatory process, and whether it occurred before a law enforcement or regulatory authority (federal, state or local authority) had already obtained knowledge regarding noncompliance. A disclosure is not considered to be "voluntary" if that disclosure is nothing more than what is already specifically required by law, regulation, or permit.

M. Extent of Company Cooperation

The prosecutor should consider the degree and timeliness of cooperation by the person/entity. Full and prompt cooperation is essential, whether in the context of a voluntary disclosure or after the government has independently learned of a violation. Consideration should be given to the violator's willingness to make all relevant information available to government investigators and prosecutors. Consideration should also be given to the extent and quality of the violator's assistance to the government's investigation. Considerable weight should also be given to prompt, good faith efforts to reach environmental compliance and remediation agreements with federal or state authorities, or both. Full compliance with such agreements should be a factor in any decision to prosecute.

III. Application of These Factors to the Case at Hand

The existence and extent of one or more of the foregoing factors as part of a voluntary compliance/audit program should be favorably considered by the prosecutor in exercising his discretion in evaluating environmental criminal cases. Situations facing prosecutors, of course, present a wide variety of fact patterns. Therefore, in a given case, some of the criteria may be satisfied while others may not. Moreover, satisfaction of various criteria may be a matter of degree. Consequently, the effect of a given mix of factors is also a matter of degree. Even if satisfaction of the criteria is not complete, still the company may benefit in terms of degree of criminal enforcement response by the government.

IV. Nature of this Policy Statement

This Policy Statement explains the current general practice of the prosecutor in making criminal prosecutive and other decisions after giving consideration to the factors described above, as well as any other factors and criteria that are relevant to the exercise of criminal prosecutorial discretion in a particular case. This discussion is an expression of, and in no way departs from, the long tradition of exercising prosecutorial discretion. The decision to prosecute rests entirely in the prosecutor's discretion. The criteria set forth above are intended only as guidance to the prosecutor in the exercise of his discretion. They are not intended to, do not, and may not be relied upon to create a right or benefit, substantive or procedural, enforceable at law by a party to litigation with the State of New Jersey, nor do they in any way limit the lawful litigative prerogatives, including civil or administrative enforcement actions, of the State of New Jersey or its Department of Environmental Protection and Energy. They are provided to guide the effective use of limited enforcement resources and do not derive from, find their basis in, nor constitute any legal requirement, whether constitutional, statutory, or otherwise, to forego or modify any enforcement action or the use of any evidentiary material.

APPENDIX C

FACTORS IN DECISIONS ON CRIMINAL PROSECUTIONS FOR ENVIRONMENTAL VIOLATIONS IN THE CONTEXT OF SIGNIFICANT VOLUNTARY COMPLIANCE OR DISCLOSURE EFFORTS BY THE VIOLATOR

U.S. DEPARTMENT OF JUSTICE

July 1, 1991

APPENDIX C

FACTORS IN DECISIONS ON CRIMINAL PROSECUTIONS FOR ENVIRONMENTAL VIOLATIONS IN THE CONTEXT OF SIGNIFICANT VOLUNTARY COMPLIANCE OR DISCLOSURE EFFORTS BY THE VIOLATOR

U.S. DEPARTMENT OF JUSTICE
JULY 1, 1991

I.   Introduction

It is the policy of the Department of Justice to encourage self-auditing, self-policing and voluntary disclosure of environmental violations by the regulated community by indicating that these activities are viewed as mitigating factors in the Department's exercise of criminal environmental enforcement discretion. This document is intended to describe the factors that the Department of Justice considers in deciding whether to bring a criminal prosecution for a violation of an environmental statute, so that such prosecutions do not create a disincentive to or undermine the goal of encouraging critical self-auditing, self-policing, and voluntary disclosure. It is designed to give federal prosecutors direction concerning the exercise of prosecutorial discretion in environmental criminal cases and to ensure that such discretion is exercised consistently nationwide. It is also intended to give the regulated community a sense of how the federal government exercises its criminal prosecutorial discretion with respect to such factors as the defendant's voluntary disclosure of violations, cooperation with the government in investigating the violations, use of environmental audits and other procedures to ensure compliance with all applicable environmental laws and regulations, and use of measures to remedy expeditiously and completely any violations and the harms caused thereby.

This guidance and the examples contained herein provide a framework for the determination of whether a particular case presents the type of circumstances in which lenience would be appropriate.

II.   Factors to be Considered

Where the law and evidence would otherwise be sufficient for prosecution, the attorney for the Department should consider the factors contained herein, to the extent they are applicable, along with any other relevant

- 122 -

factors, in determining whether and how to prosecute. It must be emphasized that these are examples of the types of factors which could be relevant. They do not constitute a definitive recipe or checklist of requirements. They merely illustrate some of the types of information which is relevant to our exercise of prosecutorial discretion.

It is unlikely that any one factor will be dispositive in any given case. All relevant factors are considered and given the weight deemed appropriate in the particular case. See <u>Federal Principles of Prosecution</u> (U.S. Dept. of Justice, 1980), Comment to Part A.2; Part B.3.

A. Voluntary Disclosure

The attorney for the Department should consider whether the person[109] made a voluntary, timely and complete disclosure of the matter under investigation. Consideration should be given to whether the person came forward promptly after discovering the noncompliance, and to the quantity and quality of information provided. Particular consideration should be given to whether the disclosure substantially aided the government's investigatory process, and whether it occurred before a law enforcement or regulatory authority (federal, state or local authority) had already obtained knowledge regarding noncompliance. A disclosure is not considered to be "voluntary" if that disclosure is already specifically required by law, regulation, or permit.[110]

B. Cooperation

The attorney for the Department should consider the degree and timeliness of cooperation by the person. Full and prompt cooperation is

---

[109] As used in this document, the terms "person" and "violator" are intended to refer to business and nonprofit entities as well as individuals.

[110] For example, any person in charge of a vessel or of an on shore facility or an offshore facility is required to notify the appropriate agency of the United States Government of any discharge of oil or a hazardous substance into or upon <u>inter alia</u> the navigable waters of the United States. Section 311(b)(5) of the Clean Water Act, 33 U.S.C. 1321(b)(5), as amended by the Oil Pollution Act of 1990, Pub. L. 101-380, § 4301(a), 104 Stat. 485, 533 (1990).

essential, whether in the context of a voluntary disclosure or after the government has independently learned of a violation. Consideration should be given to the violator's willingness to make all relevant information (including the complete results of any internal or external investigation and the names of all potential witnesses) available to government investigators and prosecutors. Consideration should also be given to the extent and quality of the violator's assistance to the government's investigation.

C. Preventive Measures and Compliance Programs

The attorney for the Department should consider the existence and scope of any regularized, intensive, and comprehensive environmental compliance program; such a program may include an environmental compliance or management audit. Particular consideration should be given to whether the compliance or audit program includes sufficient measures to identify and prevent future noncompliance, and whether the program was adopted in good faith in a timely manner.

Compliance programs may vary but the following questions should be asked in evaluating any program: Was there a strong institutional policy to comply with all environmental requirements? Had safeguards beyond those required by existing law been developed and implemented to prevent noncompliance from occurring? Were there regular procedures, including internal or external compliance and management audits, to evaluate, detect, prevent and remedy circumstances like those that led to the noncompliance? Were there procedures and safeguards to ensure the integrity of any audit conducted? Did the audit evaluate all sources of pollution (i.e., all media), including the possibility of cross-media transfers of pollutants? Were the auditor's recommendations implemented in a timely fashion? Were adequate resources committed to the auditing program and to implementing its recommendations? Was environmental compliance a standard by which employee and corporate departmental performance was judged?

D. Additional Factors Which May Be Relevant

1. Pervasiveness of Noncompliance

Pervasive noncompliance may indicate systemic or repeated participation in or condonation of criminal behavior. It may also indicate the lack of a meaningful compliance program. In evaluating this factor, the attorney for the

Department should consider, among other things, the number and level of employees participating in the unlawful activities and the obviousness, seriousness, duration, history, and frequency of noncompliance.

2. Internal Disciplinary Action

Effective internal disciplinary action is crucial to any compliance program. The attorney for the Department should consider whether there was an effective system of discipline for employees who violated company environmental compliance policies. Did the disciplinary system establish an awareness in other employees that unlawful conduct would not be condoned?

3. Subsequent Compliance Efforts

The attorney for the Department should consider the extent of any efforts to remedy any ongoing noncompliance. The promptness and completeness of any action taken to remove the source of the noncompliance and to lessen the environmental harm resulting from the noncompliance should be considered. Considerable weight should be given to prompt, good-faith efforts to reach environmental compliance agreements with federal or state authorities, or both. Full compliance with such agreements should be a factor in any decision whether to prosecute.

III. Application of These Factors to Hypothetical Examples[111]

These examples are intended to assist federal prosecutors in their exercise of discretion in evaluating environmental cases. The situations facing prosecutors, of course, present a wide variety of fact patterns. Therefore, in a given case, some of the criteria may be satisfied while others may not. Moreover, satisfaction of various criteria may be a matter of degree. Consequently, the effect of a given mix of factors also is a matter of degree. In the ideal situation, if a company fully meets all of the criteria, the result may be a decision not to prosecute that company criminally. Even if satisfaction of the criteria is not complete, still the company may benefit in terms of degree of

---

[111] While this policy applies to both individuals and organizational violators, these examples focus particularly upon situations involving organizations.

enforcement response by the government. The following hypothetical examples are intended to illustrate the operation of these guidelines.

Example 1:

This is the ideal case in terms of criteria satisfaction and consequent prosecution leniency.

1. Company A regularly conducts a comprehensive audit of its compliance with environmental requirements.

2. The audit uncovers information about employees' disposing of hazardous wastes by dumping them in an unpermitted location.

3. An internal company investigation confirms the audit information. (Depending upon the nature of the audit, this follow-up investigation may be unnecessary.)

4. Prior to the violations the company had a sound compliance program, which included clear policies, employee training, and a hotline for suspected violations.

5. As soon as the company confirms the violations, it discloses all pertinent information to the appropriate government agency; it undertakes compliance planning with that agency; and it carries out satisfactory remediation measures.

6. The company also undertakes to correct any false information previously submitted to the government in relation to the violations.

7. Internally the company disciplines the employees actually involved in the violations, including any supervisor who was lax in preventing or detecting the activity. Also, the company reviews its compliance program to determine how the violations slipped by and corrects the weaknesses found by that review.

8. The company discloses to the government the names of the employees actually responsible for the violations, and it cooperates with the government by providing documentation necessary to the investigation of those persons.

Under these circumstances Company A would stand a good chance of being favorably considered for prosecutorial leniency, to the extent of not being criminally prosecuted at all. The degree of any leniency, however, may turn upon other relevant factors not specifically dealt with in these guidelines.[112/]

Example 2:

At the opposite end of the scale is Company Z, which meets few of the criteria. The likelihood of prosecutorial leniency, therefore, is remote. Company Z's circumstances may include any of the following:

1. Because an employee has threatened to report a violation to federal authorities, the company is afraid that investigators may begin looking at it. An audit is undertaken, but its focuses only upon the particular violation, ignoring the possibility that the violation may be indicative of widespread activities in the organization.

2. After completing the audit, Company Z reports the violations discovered to the government.

3. The company had a compliance program, but it was effectively no more than a collection of paper. No effort is made to disseminate its content, impress upon employees its significance, train employees in its application, or oversee its implementation.

4. Even after "discovery" of the violation the company makes no effort to strengthen its compliance procedures.

5. The company makes no effort to come to terms with regulators regarding its violations. It resists any remedial work and refuses to pay any monetary sanctions.

[112/] For example, if the company had a long history of noncompliance, the compliance audit was done only under pressure from regulators, and a timely audit would have ended the violations much sooner, those circumstances would be considered.

6. Because of the non-compliance, information submitted to regulators over the years has been materially inaccurate, painting a substantially false picture of the company's true compliance situation. The company fails to take any steps to correct that inaccuracy.

7. The company does not cooperate with prosecutors in identifying those employees (including managers) who actually were involved in the violation, and it resists disclosure of any documents relating either to the violations or to the responsible employees.

In these circumstances leniency is unlikely. The only positive action is the so-called audit, but that was so narrowly focused as to be of questionable value, and it was undertaken only to head off a possible criminal investigation. Otherwise, the company demonstrated no good faith either in terms of compliance efforts or in assisting the government in obtaining a full understanding of the violation and discovering its sources.

Nonetheless, these factors do not assure a criminal prosection of Company Z. As with Company A, above, other circumstances may be present which affect the balance struck by prosecutors. For example, the effect of the violation (because of substance, duration, or amount) may be such that prosecutors would not consider it to be an appropriate criminal case. Administrative or civil proceedings may be considered a more appropriate response.

Other examples:

Between these extremes there is a range of possibilities. The presence, absence, or degree of any criterion may affect the prosecution's exercise of discretion. Below are some examples of such effects:

1. In a situation otherwise similar to that of Company A, above, Company B performs an audit that is very limited in scope and probably reflects no more than an effort to avoid prosection. Despite that background, Company B is cooperative in terms of both bringing itself into compliance and providing information regarding the crime and its perpetrators. The result could be any of a number of outcomes, including prosecution of a lesser charge or a decision to prosecute the individuals rather than the company.

2. Again the situation is similar to Company A's, but Company C refuses to reveal any information regarding the individual violators. The likelihood of the government's prosecuting the company are substantially increased.

3. In another situation similar to Company A's, Company D chooses to "sit on" the audit and take corrective action without telling the government. The government learns of the situation months or years after the fact.

    A complicating fact here is that environmental regulatory programs are self policing: they include a substantial number of reporting requirements. If reports which in fact presented false information are allowed to stand uncorrected, the reliability of this system is undermined. They also may lead to adverse and unfair impacts upon other members of the regulated community. For example, Company D failed to report discharges of X contaminant into a municipal sewer system, discharges that were terminated as a result of an audit. The sewer authority, though, knowing only that there have been excessive loadings of X, but not knowing that company D was a source, tightens limitations upon all known sources of X. Thus, all of those sources incur additional treatment expenses, but Company D is unaffected. Had Company D revealed its audit results, the other companies would not have suffered unnecessary expenses.

    In some situations, moreover, failure to report is a crime. See, e.g., 33 U.S.C. § 1321(b)(5) and 42 U.S.C. § 9603(b). To illustrate the effect of this factor, consider Company E, which conducts a thorough audit and finds that hazardous wastes have been disposed of by dumping them on the ground. The company cleans up the area and tightens up its compliance program, but does not reveal the situation to regulators. Assuming that a reportable quantity of a hazardous substance was released, the company was under a legal obligation under 42 U.S.C. § 9603(b) to report that release as soon as it had knowledge of it, thereby allowing regulators the opportunity to assure proper clean up. Company E's knowing failure to report the release upon learning of it is itself a felony.

In the cases of both Company D and Company E, consideration would be given by prosecutors for remedial efforts; hence prosecution of fewer or lesser charges might result. However, because Company D's silence adversely affected others who are entitled to fair regulatory treatment and because Company E deprived those legally responsible for evaluating cleanup needs of the ability to carry out their functions, the likelihood of their totally escaping criminal prosecution is significantly reduced.

4. Company F's situation is similar to that of Company B. However, with regard to the various violations shown by the audit, it concentrates upon correcting only the easier, less expensive, less significant among them. Its lackadaisical approach to correction does not make it a strong candidate for leniency.

5. Company G is similar to Company D in that it performs an audit and finds violations, but does not bring them to the government's attention. Those violations do not involve failures to comply with reporting requirements. The company undertakes a program of gradually correcting its violations. When the government learns of the situation, Company G still has not remedied its most significant violations, but claims that it certainly planned to get to them. Company G could receive some consideration for its efforts, but its failure to disclose and the slowness of its remedial work probably mean that it cannot expect a substantial degree of leniency.

6. Comprehensive audits are considered positive efforts toward good faith compliance. However, such audits are not indispensable to enforcement leniency. Company H's situation is essentially identical to that of Company A, except for the fact that it does not undertake a comprehensive audit. It does not have a formal audit program, but, as a part of its efforts to ensure compliance, does realize that it is committing an environmental violation. It hereafter takes steps otherwise identical to those of Company A in terms of compliance efforts and cooperation. Company H is also a likely candidate for leniency, including possibly no criminal prosecution.

In sum, mitigating efforts made by the regulated community will be recognized and evaluated. The greater the showing of good faith, the more likely it will be met with leniency. Conversely, the less good faith shown, the less likely that prosecutorial discretion will tend toward leniency.

IV.   Nature of this Guidance

This guidance explains the current general practice of the Department in making criminal prosecutive and other decisions after giving consideration to the criteria described above, as well as any other criteria that are relevant to the exercise of criminal prosecutorial discretion in a particular case. This discussion is an expression of, and in no way departs from, the long tradition of exercising prosecutorial discretion. The decision to prosecute "generally rests entirely in [the prosecutor's] discretion." Bordenkircher v. Hayes, 434 U.S. 357, 364 (1978).[113] This discretion is especially firmly held by the criminal prosecutor.[114] The criteria set forth above are intended only as internal guidance to Department of Justice attorneys. They are not intended to, do not, and may not be relied upon to create a right or benefit, substantive or procedural, enforceable at law by a party to litigation with the United States, nor do they in any way limit the lawful litigative prerogatives, including civil enforcement actions, of the Department of Justice or the Environmental Protection Agency. They are provided to guide the effective use of limited enforcement resources, and do not derive from, find their basis in, nor constitute any legal requirement, whether constitutional, statutory, or otherwise, to forego or modify any enforcement action or the use of evidentiary material. See Principles of Federal Prosecution (U.S. Dept. of Justice, 1980) p. 4; United States Attorneys' Manual (U.S. Dept. of Justice, 1986) 1-1.000.

---

[113]   Although some statutes have occasionally been held to require civil enforcement actions, see, e.g., Dunlop v. Bachowski, 421 U.S. 560 (1975), those are unusual cases, and the general rule is that both civil and criminal enforcement is at the enforcement agency's discretion where not prescribed by law. Heckler v. Chaney, 470 U.S. 821, 830-35 (1985); Cutler v. Hayes, 818 F.2d 879, 893 (D.C. Cir. 1987) (decisions not to enforce are not reviewable unless the statute provides an "inflexible mandate").

[114]   Newman v. United States, 382 F.2d 479, 480 (D.C. Cir. 1967).

APPENDIX D

**WORKING DRAFT RECOMMENDATIONS BY THE ADVISORY
WORKING GROUP ON ENVIRONMENTAL SANCTIONS
TO THE UNITED STATES SENTENCING COMMISSION**

U.S. DEPARTMENT OF JUSTICE

APPENDIX D

WORKING DRAFT RECOMMENDATIONS BY THE ADVISORY WORKING GROUP ON ENVIRONMENTAL SANCTIONS TO THE UNITED STATES SENTENCING COMMISSION

STEP I:
BASE FINE

a. The base fine is the greater of:

 (1) the economic gain plus costs directly attributable to the offense; or

 (2) a percentage, derived from the Base Fine Table below, of the maximum statutory fine that could be imposed for the offenses of conviction.

BASE FINE TABLE

OFFENSE TYPE	PERCENTAGE OF MAXIMUM STATUTORY FINE
(a) An offense involving knowing endangerment (under the Resource Conservation and Recovery Act, Clean Water Act, or Clean Air Act)	90-100 %
(b) An offense involving unlawful handling of a hazardous substance or other environmental pollutant resulting in an actual release, discharge, disposal or emission into the environment	60-90 %

(c) An offense involving unlawful   40-70 %
handling of a hazardous substance
or other environmental pollutant creating a
material threat of actual release, discharge,
disposal or emission into the environment

(d) An offense involving knowing   30-50 %
falsification; knowing concealment or
destruction; knowing omission or tampering

(e) Other offenses involving   15-30 %
unlawful handling of a hazardous substance
or other environmental pollutant not
resulting in an actual or threatened
release, discharge, disposal or emission
into the environment

(f) Wildlife offense   __-__ %

(g) An offense involving simple   10-20 %
recordkeeping and reporting

b. [Where the court finds that the Base Fine calculated pursuant to Step I(a) would be unjust as a result of the unnecessary or excessive repetition of counts relating to a course of offense behavior that is ongoing or continuous in nature and does not involve independent volitional acts, the court may, in the interest of justice, reduce the Base Fine by deleting the unnecessary or repetitious counts from its computation of the Base Fine. In so doing, the court should insure that the Base Fine adequately reflects the seriousness of the offense, the culpability of the defendant and each of the distinct types of criminal violations involved.][115]

---

[115]   This provision presented a particularly difficult issue upon which opinion was sharply divided. Accordingly, public comment is solicited as to whether Step I(b) should be included.

Commentary

Statutory Provisions: 7 U.S.C. §§ 136-1361; 15 U.S.C. §§ 2614 and 2615; 33 U.S.C. §§ 403, 406, 407, 411; 1319(c), 1907, 1908, 1321(b)(5), 1415(b), 1517; 42 U.S.C. §§ 300(h) - 2, 6928(d) and (e), 7413(c), 9603(b), (c), and (d), 11045(4) and (d)(2), 43 U.S.C. §§ 1350, 1816(a), 1822(b), 49 U.S.C. §§ 1804, and 1809. For additional statutory provisions, <u>see</u> Appendix A (Statutory Index), United States Sentencing Commission Guideline Manual (November 1, 1992).

Application Notes

1. Determinations under this chapter are to be based on the provisions of the guidelines in this chapter. Determinations that reference other chapters are to be made under the standards set forth in those chapters. Also incorporated by reference in this chapter are guidelines 1B1.1 (application notes b and j), 1B1.2, 1B1.4, 1B1.5, 1B1.7, 1B1.8, 1B1.9, 1B1.11, 5E1.3, 6A1.1, 6A1.2, 6A1.3, 6B1.1, 6B1.2, 6B1.3, 6B1.4, Application Note 3(a) - (j) inclusive to Section 8A1.2, 8B1.1, 8B1.2, 8B1.3.

2. Where the offenses of conviction include counts governed by this chapter as well as counts governed by other chapters, determine the fines for environmental offenses and non-environmental offenses separately. Where the offenses are closely interrelated as defined in Section 3D1.2, whether or not they involve the same act or transaction, then the fine should be based on the greater of the environmental or the non-environmental offense fine and adjusted to take into account the specific offense or offender characteristics of the lesser-fined offense. For example, when the non-environmental count embodies conduct properly treated as a specific offense characteristic or adjustment to the guidelines determination for the environmental offense and is connected by a common criminal objective or common scheme or plan, treat the offenses as "closely interrelated." Where the environmental and non-environmental offenses are not closely interrelated the fines should be cumulative.

3. "Economic gain" referred to in Step I(a)(1) is defined as 1) the economic benefits that an offender realized by avoiding or delaying capital costs necessary to comply with the environmental statute, based upon the estimated cost of capital to the offender; 2) the continuing expenses (e.g., labor, energy, leases, operation and maintenance) the offender avoided or delayed by noncompliance; and 3) other profits directly attributable to the offense conduct which is described in the criminal charges.

4. The "costs" referred to in Step I(a)(1) include the following provided they are reasonably quantifiable: 1) actual environmental harm, proximately caused by the offense conduct including material degradation of a natural resource, and 2) harms incurred and remediation or other costs borne by others. If any component of such costs cannot be determined, the remaining determinable component shall be used for measuring environmental costs. "Material degradation" is the causing of, or contribution to, the extended or widespread impairment of the condition or usage of a natural resource. "Natural resource" includes land (whether surface or subsurface), fish, wildlife, biota, air, water, and drinking water supplies.

5. The factor of harm or risk of harm to the environment (as distinct from releases or threats of releases) is addressed in Step I only to the extent the costs of actual harm are reasonably quantifiable under Step I(a)(1). Accordingly, except to the extent the costs of harm have been calculated under Step I(a)(1), the court shall consider harm or risk of harm under Step II.

6. Each percentage figure is multiplied by the statutory maximum fine for that count according to 18 U.S.C. § 3571(c) without giving effect to 18 U.S.C. § 3571(d).

7. In calculating a base fine under Step I(a)(2), in cases with convictions for more than one type of environmental violation, the court shall calculate the base fine as the sum of the fine for each individual conviction. Accordingly, if a defendant has been convicted of three counts (one each under Step I(a)(2)(b), (c), and (d)), the court shall first determine the appropriate percentage of the statutory fine for each of the three counts. The sum of these three individual figures

will serve as the base fine under Step I(a). The offense will be treated as a group for calculations under Step II, III, IV, and V. For any count of conviction (involving lesser included offenses), the court should apply the highest Step I(a)(2) category applicable to the offense.

8. In determining whether there was an actual or threatened release, discharge, disposal, or emission of a hazardous substance or other environmental pollutant into the environment, the court should refer to the applicable statutory and regulatory definitions relating to the statute under which the defendant was convicted.

9. Subsection (a)(2)(b) includes, but is not limited to, the following situations: 1) unlawful treatment of a hazardous waste when the resulting waste material is released into the environment; 2) unlawful export or transportation of hazardous substances when it cannot be determined that it was properly disposed of; 3) violations of work practice standards under the Clean Air Act; 4) falsifications, knowing omissions or tamperings that conceal an actual release, discharge, disposal or emission of a hazardous substance or pollutant into the environment; 5) releases of hazardous substances or other environmental pollutants while failing to operate properly required measurement or monitoring equipment; and 6) knowing failure to report releases in violation of EPCRTKA, CERCLA or the Clean Water Act.

10. Subsection (a)(2)(d) includes, but is not limited to a conviction for failure to provide notification of a demolition or renovation involving asbestos regulated under the Clean Air Act.

11. A violation presents a material threat of a release if it creates circumstances where a release is more than a remote or hypothetical possibility.

12. "Simple recordkeeping or reporting violations" under Step I(a)(2)(g) are limited to situations where the defendant neither knew nor had reason to believe that the recordkeeping or reporting offense would

significantly increase the likelihood of any substantive environmental harm.

13. The Base Fine Table establishes the ranges, expressed in percentages of the maximum statutory fine, that could be imposed for the offense of conviction. These ranges allow the court a limited degree of discretion in setting the appropriate percentage for a given offense. The court's selection of a given percentage within the applicable range shall be based on the relative gravity of the offense. Factors to be taken into account in determining gravity include: the particular amount of hazardous substance or other environmental pollutant; the relative toxicity of the hazardous substance or other environmental pollutant; and the extent to which an applicable environmental standard, guideline or condition was exceeded.

For example:

> If the violation involved a hazardous substance, the lower that substance's reportable quantity listed in 40 C.F.R. § 302.4 the higher in the range the base fine should be set;

> If the offense caused the evacuation or disruption of a public utility, then the base fine should fall at the high end of the range;

> If the offense involved the release into the environment of a hazardous substance listed in 40 C.F.R. § 302.4 and its reportable quantity was actually exceeded, the base fine should fall at the high end of the range;

> If the offense involved damage to wetlands or other sensitive habitats, the court should take into account both the size and value of the wetlands or habitat impacted in determining the appropriate base fine within the range.

Comment 1: Step I does not follow the procedures for grouping multiple counts set forth in Chapter 3D, which in the case of "closely interrelated" offenses bases the sentence on the offense level for the most serious offense in that group. See § 3D1.3(a). Applied to environmental offenses, this approach could understate the harm that environmental crimes can cause. Thus, Step I does not group environmental offenses, and instead requires the court to consider the aggregate economic gain and environmental costs from each offense of conviction. However, because this alternative approach may create the possibility of inappropriate count proliferation to increase the fine under Step I(a)(2), Step I(b) authorizes the court to reduce repetitious or excessive counts to prevent a disproportionate Base Fine. For example, if an organization committed a storage offense by failing to segregate certain toxic materials or wastes that it did not realize required such special storage and this conduct continued over a year or more, the Base Fine would be disproportionate to the organization's culpability if each day during this period was charged as a separate offense. Similarly, the negligent discharge of a non-toxic pollutant into a river over a period of several months as the result of a leaky pipe valve (where no responsible corporate manager was aware of this continuing discharge) should not normally be punished as a separate offense for each day during this period. Rather, in each case, the court should reduce the counts for sentencing purposes to a representative number.

Comment 2: No reduction in the number of counts is authorized under Step I(b) where the conduct involved "independent volitional acts." Thus, it would be inappropriate to reduce the number of counts for sentencing purposes in a case where an organization intentionally discharged pollutants into a river over a sustained period (for example, as the result of knowingly using a hidden bypass valve). The failure to rectify the problem, once it became known, should be viewed as committing "independent" volitional acts. In addition, if the organization has been clearly negligent in failing to detect the continuing discharge, this factor should also be considered by the court in determining whether and to what extent it should reduce the number of counts for purposes of computing the Base Fine.

Comment 3: The authority conferred by Step I(b) should be used sparingly. Any reduction under Step I(b) should not be below the level deemed by the court as necessary to adequately reflect the seriousness of the total offense conduct and each of the various types of misbehavior.

Questions for public comment:

1)   Comment is solicited on whether costs should be included in determining the base fine as provided in Step I(a)(1).

2)   Comment is solicited on whether, if costs are so included, these costs should include material degradation of a natural resource.

3)   Comment is solicited on whether, if costs are so included, the harms incurred and costs borne by others should be included.

4)   Comment is solicited on whether there are other factors that should be included in the determination of the base fine (e.g. human health effects).

5)   Comment is solicited on whether the costs in Step I(a)(1) should include not only the costs borne by others but also costs borne by the defendant.

6)   Comment is solicited on whether Step I(a)(2) should have a specific percentage of the maximum statutory fine set or allow a range (as currently drafted).

7)   Comment is solicited on the most appropriate range for the percentage of the statutory maximum for wildlife violations.

8)   Comment is solicited on whether Step I(b) should be included.

STEP II:
AGGRAVATING FACTORS IN SENTENCING

(a)   **Management Involvement**

If one or more members of the substantial authority personnel of the organization participated in, condoned, solicited, or concealed the criminal conduct, or recklessly tolerated conditions or circumstances that created or perpetuated a significant risk that criminal behavior of the same general type or kind would occur or continue, increase the Base Fine by ___% to ___%. If a corporate manager lacking the authority or responsibility to be classified as a member of the organization's substantial authority personnel, but having supervisory responsibility to detect, prevent, or abate the violation, engaged in the criminal conduct, increase the Base Fine by ___% to ___%.

Commentary

Comment: The term "substantial authority personnel" is defined in application note 3(c) to § 8A1.2. The determination of an individual employee's status within the organization should be made on a case-by-case basis. However, for the purposes of environmental sanctions, plant managers and senior environmental compliance personnel will almost invariably be deemed "substantial authority personnel." In determining the extent to apply this factor under this provision, the court should look to the extent, duration and pervasiveness of any managerial involvement and the level of the specific employee involved. Although the determination of an employee's status within the organization must be done on a case-by-case basis, personnel such as loading dock foremen or night watchmen would ordinarily not be classified as corporate managers having supervisory responsibility to detect, prevent, or abate violations, even if in fact they possessed some preventive capability.

(b)   **Threat to the Environment**

If the organization (i) caused actual and identifiable harm to the environment that materially degraded a natural resource, or (ii) knowingly created a significant risk of material degradation of a natural resource, increase the Base Fine by ___% to ___%.

Commentary

Comment: For the definition of "materially degraded," refer to Application Note 4 under Step I. This factor should be considered only to the extent that it is not taken into account in the calculation under Step I(a)(1).

(c) **Threat to Human Life or Safety**

If the organization (i) caused death or serious bodily injury, or (ii) knowingly created a significant risk of such harm, increase the Base Fine by ___% to ___%.

Commentary

Comment: The threat to human life or safety should be considered only to the extent that it is not taken into account in the calculation under Step I(a)(1).

(d) **Scienter**

If employees or agents of the corporation knowingly engaged in conduct that violated the law under circumstances that evidenced at least a reckless indifference to legal requirements, increase the base Fine by ___% to ___%.

Commentary

Comment: Ignorance of the law is rarely an excuse. However, when the offender is aware of or indifferent to the criminal character of the conduct, such scienter is an aggravating factor that increases the culpability of the offense. In determining the amount by which to enhance the fine under Step II(d), the court should consider such factors as: (1) the level of intent (a knowing and willful intent to violate the law merits the greatest enhancement, while reckless behavior undertaken with awareness of the possibility that it was unlawful would merit a lesser increase); (2) the level of the employee within the organization possessing the requisite state of mind (where awareness of probable unlawfulness can be attributed to substantial authority personnel, the enhancement may appropriately be raised to or near the maximum authorized by this provision); (3) the pervasiveness of the awareness or knowledge; and (4) whether the individual acting with knowledge or awareness of actual or probable illegality was primarily pursuing personal, non-organizational policies (the so-called "rogue employee"), in which case no or minimum enhancement would be appropriate. There shall be a presumption that high level personnel are not considered rogue employees. Knowledge or awareness of probable illegality will normally have to be inferred by the court from circumstantial evidence. Covert or evasive behavior is often an indication of such knowledge or awareness.

(e)   **Prior Criminal Compliance History**

If the organization committed any part of the instant offense less than 5 years after a criminal adjudication of violation of federal or state environmental law, increase the Base Fine by ___% to ___%, but if the prior adjudication is for similar misconduct, increase the Base Fine by ___% to ___%.

Commentary

Comment 1: A prior criminal adjudication includes an adjudication of an offense which occurs at the same or a different location or facility, and includes convictions under Title 18 where the underlying behavior involves noncompliance with environmental statutes or regulations, e.g., 371, 1001, 1341. "Similar misconduct" includes similar actions or omissions at the same or a different location or facility and without regard to whether such prior misconduct was adjudged a violation of the same statutory provision as the instant offense.

Comment 2: For purposes of Step II(e) and (f), the term organization includes subsidiaries (including subsidiaries where the ownership is less than 100%) where the subsidiary is not "separately managed" by independent management. See also Comments 5 and 6 to Application Notes to § 8C2.5. For example, assume that XYZ, Inc. is the largest single shareholder with 51% of the XYZ Shipping Company, whose operations largely consist of shipping petroleum products for XYZ, Inc. and whose officers report to XYZ's management. On these facts, XYZ's prior civil and criminal history would include both criminal convictions and civil or administrative adjudications of XYZ Shipping Company.

(f) **Prior Civil Compliance History**

If the number, severity, or pattern of the organization's prior civil or administrative adjudications within the five years prior to the date of the instant conviction, when considered in light of the size, scope and character of the organization and its operations, reveals a disregard by the organization of its environmental regulatory responsibilities, increase the Base Fine by ___% to ___%, but if a prior civil or administrative adjudication is for similar misconduct, increase the Base Fine by ___% to ___%.

Commentary

Comment 1: Under this provision the court should undertake a qualitative assessment of the organization's prior environmental regulatory history over the five years prior to the instant conviction. Because organizations differ materially in the size and scope of their operations, a simple mechanical counting rule for past adjudications has been rejected. For some organizations, because of their scale or constant involvement with environmental regulation, a prior history of civil or administrative adjudications may neither show special culpability nor merit any significant enhancement of the Base Fine under this provision. Conversely, a prior serious violation or a pattern of less serious adjudications (even by a very large organization) may show inattention to the organization's regulatory responsibilities or even a willingness to accept fines as a cost of doing business. In either case, this would indicate the need for enhancement of the penalty. An organization's prior history may also indicate types of offenses that it should have taken special care to prevent. The recurrence of similar misconduct can be highly probative evidence of an organization's disregard of its corporate responsibility and its failure to take all necessary steps to prevent continued misconduct.

Comment 2: A prior administrative or civil adjudication includes an adjudication of an offense which occurs at the same or different location or facility. "Similar misconduct" includes similar actions or omissions at the same or different location or facility and without regard to whether such prior misconduct was adjudged a violation of the same statutory provision as the instant offense.

(g) **Concealment**

If any employee or agent of the organization sought to conceal the violation or to obstruct administrative, civil, or criminal investigation of the violation by knowingly furnishing inaccurate material information or by knowingly omitting material information, increase the Base Fine by ___% to ___%.

Commentary

Comment: This aggravator is primarily directed at conduct engaged in during the course of an investigation. In any event, this aggravator would not apply to offenses treated under Step I(a)(2)(d) where the predicate offense involves the same concealment conduct. This aggravating factor relates to non-privileged information that is either required by law to be furnished or given voluntarily by any employee or agent of an organization to a federal, state or local official or agency. It includes information furnished in either written or oral form. The provision is not to be construed as a disclosure requirement where none otherwise exists; however, if disclosure is either legally required or voluntarily made, knowing efforts to mislead regulatory authorities by furnishing inaccurate material information or omitting material information shall be a basis for increasing the fine level. Such efforts include indirect concealment, for example, where A provides information directly to B, who then uses A's information in preparing a submission to EPA. A either gives B inaccurate material information or omits material information in an effort to conceal a violation from the government. If A knows that his act will cause B (an unwitting player in this example) to mislead regulatory authorities, the aggravator applies.

(h) **Violation of an Order**

If the commission of the instant offense violated a judicial order or injunction (other than a condition of probation), an administrative order, a cease and desist order, or occurs following a notice of violation for the same offense conduct, increase the Base Fine by ___% to ___%.

Commentary

Comment: The amount by which the Base Fine is increased will depend upon the type of order issued to, and violated by, the defendant (e.g. judicial v. administrative), and the degree of contempt exhibited by the defendant.

(i) **Absence of Compliance Program or Other Organized Effort**

If, prior to the offense, the organization either had no program or other organized effort to achieve and maintain compliance with environmental requirements, or it had such a program in form only and had substantially failed to implement such a program, increase the Base Fine by ___% to ___%.

Commentary

Comment 1: To establish a basis for avoiding aggravation of the Base Fine under this provision, the organization must document the existence of some form of program or other organized effort to achieve and maintain compliance. To establish a basis for aggravation of the Base Fine under Step II(i), the prosecution must carry the burden of demonstrating that the organization substantially failed to implement a program or other organized effort to achieve and maintain compliance.

Comment 2: "Environmental requirements" include all legally enforceable environmental compliance obligations imposed by federal, state or local statute, regulation, permit, judicial or administrative decree, order and agreement, or other similar means.

Comment 3: In order to evaluate an organization's environmental compliance program or other organized effort, the court may utilize experts as specified in Comment 4 to Step III.

(j)   **Absence of a Permit**

If the conduct underlying commission of the instant offense occurred
without a requisite permit, increase the Base Fine by ___% to ___%.[116]

Commentary

Comment: Reference to a permit includes any permit or license, or its
equivalent which may be required under federal, state or local pollution
abatement programs. For example, this provision would include a permit
for a tie-in to a municipal or regional sewage treatment system; a
manifest for the transportation of hazardous waste; a foreign country's
consent for the export of hazardous waste; or an international agreement
governing the export of hazardous waste. This provision also applies to
situations covered by a federal, state or local permit, but where the
permitting authority would never issue a permit for the type of conduct in
question. For example, this provision would apply to the discharge of a
load of solvents by a tanker into a navigable water; or the dumping of
drums of hazardous waste on the side of a road.

---

[116]   The Group was divided as to whether (1) this provision should be included
as an aggravator, (2) whether it is better dealt with as a basis, in Application Note
13 to Step I, for setting a base fine at the high end of the range, or (3) whether it
should be eliminated entirely. Comment is solicited on any of these three
questions.

MITIGATING FACTORS IN SENTENCING

(k)   <u>Commitment to Environmental Compliance</u>

If the organization demonstrates that, prior to the offense, it had committed the resources and the management processes that were reasonably determined to be sufficient, given its size and the nature of its business, to achieve and maintain compliance with environmental requirements, including detection and deterrence of criminal conduct by its employees or agents, reduce the Base Fine by ___% to ___%. If an individual within high-level personnel of the organization participated in, condoned, or was willfully ignorant of the offense, there shall be a rebuttable presumption that the organization had not made a commitment sufficient to achieve and maintain compliance with environmental requirements as described in Step III. In order to grant any mitigation under this provision, the court must conclude that all of the factors described in Step III were substantially satisfied.

<u>Commentary</u>

<u>Comment:</u> "High-level personnel of the organization" is defined in the Commentary to § 8A1.2 (Application Instructions - Organizations).

(l)   <u>Cooperation and Self-Reporting</u>

(1) If the organization (a) prior to an imminent threat of disclosure or government investigation, and (b) within a reasonable prompt time after becoming aware of the offense, reported the offense to appropriate governmental authorities, fully cooperated in the investigation and clearly demonstrated recognition of its responsibility and took all reasonable steps to assess responsibility within the organization and prevent recurrence, reduce the Base Fine by ___% to ___%; provided, however, that no credit shall be given where reporting of the offense was otherwise required by federal law.

(2) If the organization pleaded guilty before the government was put to substantial effort or expense in preparing for trial, fully cooperated with the prosecution, and took all reasonable steps to assess responsibility within the organization and prevent recurrence, reduce the Base Fine by ___% to ___%.

(3) If the organization pleaded guilty before the prosecution was put to substantial effort or expense in preparing for trial and cooperated with the prosecution in all relevant respects except by failing to disclose the names and identities of responsible individuals known to it (or names and identities that it could have reasonably ascertained), reduce the Base Fine by ___% to ___%.

Commentary

Comment: As used in this provision, "fully cooperated" with the prosecution includes providing the names and identities of all individuals and other persons known or reasonably ascertainable to the organization whose conduct may be relevant to the underlying offense conduct. This would include both officers and employees within the organization, outside agents, individuals within other organizations, and other co-conspirators. To "fully cooperate," the organization must also provide all pertinent information known to or ascertainable by it that would assist law enforcement personnel in identifying the nature and extent of the offense. See Comment 12 to Application Notes to § 8C2.5. Failing such cooperation in identifying potentially responsible individuals or other persons, the organization may receive only the sentencing reduction under this provision provided for in subclause (3) above. If the organization's cooperation meets the standards described in more than one provision of this provision, apply the provision with the largest Base Fine reduction.

(m) **Absence of Scienter**

If the criminal conduct was the result of negligent errors or omissions or was imposed on the basis of strict liability or collective knowledge and no corporate employee or agent acted with a level of intent at least equal to that of reckless indifference, reduce the Base Fine by ___% to ___%.

(n) **Remedial Assistance**

If the organization takes prompt action to provide assistance (in addition to any legally required restitution or remediation) to the victims of its crime to mitigate their loses, reduce the Base Fine by ___% to ___%.

Questions for public comment:

1) Comment is solicited as to the appropriate classification of consent decrees under Step II(f) and whether they should be viewed as a prior adjudication for purposes of this provision.

2) Comment is solicited on whether, if Step II(j) is eliminated, an aggravator should be added to increase the Base Fine in cases where the offender by its conduct demonstrates substantial disregard of its obligations to operate within the applicable regulatory framework designed for the protection of human health or the environment.

3) Comment is solicited as to whether mitigation credit should be given under Step II(1) absent full disclosure of all documents, statements or other material, including privileged information.

4) Comment is solicited on whether Step II(n) provides an undue benefit.

STEP III:
FACTORS FOR ENVIRONMENTAL COMPLIANCE

The court must conclude that the following factors were substantially satisfied, at a minimum, in determining that the organization has made a commitment to environmental compliance.

(a) **Line Management Attention to Compliance.** In the day-to-day operation of the organization, line managers, including the executive and operating officers at all levels, direct their attention, through the routine management mechanisms utilized throughout the organization (e.g. objective setting, progress reports, operating performance reviews, departmental meetings), to measuring, maintaining and improving the organization's compliance with environmental laws and regulation. Line managers routinely review environmental monitoring and auditing reports, direct the resolution of identified compliance issues, and ensure application of the resources and mechanisms necessary to carry out a substantial commitment.

(b) **Integration of Environmental Policies, Standards and Procedures.** The organization has adopted, and communicated to its employees and agents, policies, standards and procedures necessary to achieve environmental compliance, including a requirement that employees report any suspected violation to appropriate officials within the organization, and that a record will be kept by the organization of any such reports. To the maximum extent possible given the nature of its business, the organization has analyzed and designed the work functions (e.g. through standard operating procedures) assigned to its employees and agents so that compliance will be achieved, verified and documented in the course of performing the routine work of the organization.

(c) **Auditing, Monitoring, Reporting and Tracking Systems.** The organization has designed and implemented, with sufficient authority, personnel and other resources, the systems and programs that are necessary for:

(i)   frequent auditing (with appropriate independence from line management) and inspection (including random, and, when necessary, surprise audits and inspections) of its principal operations and all pollution control facilities to assess, in detail, their compliance with all applicable environmental requirements and the organization's internal policies, standards and procedures, as well as internal investigations and implementation of appropriate, follow-up countermeasures with respect to all significant incidents of noncompliance;

(ii)   continuous on-site monitoring, by specifically trained compliance personnel and by other means, of key operations and pollution control facilities that are either subject to significant environmental regulation, or where the nature or history of such operations or facilities suggests a significant potential for non-compliance;

(iii)   internal reporting (e.g. hotlines), without fear of retribution, of potential non-compliance to those responsible for investigating and correcting such incidents;

(iv)   tracking the status of responses to identified compliance issues to enable expeditious, effective and documented resolution of environmental compliance issues by line management; and

(v)   redundant, independent checks on the status of compliance, particularly in those operations, facilities or processes where the organization knows, or has reason to believe, that employees or agents may have, in the past, concealed non-compliance through falsification or other means, and in those operations, facilities or processes where the organization reasonably believes such potential exists.

(d) **Regulatory Expertise, Training and Evaluation.** The organization has developed and implemented, consistent with the size and nature of its business, systems or programs that are adequate to:

(i)   maintain up-to-date, sufficiently detailed understanding of all applicable environmental requirements by those employees and agents whose responsibilities require such knowledge;

(ii)   train, evaluate, and document the training and evaluation, of all employees and agents of the organization, both upon entry into the organization and on a refresher basis, as to the applicable environmental requirements, policies, standards (including ethical standards) and procedures necessary to carry out their responsibilities in compliance with those requirements, policies and standards; and

(iii)   evaluate employees and agents sufficiently to avoid delegating significant discretionary authority or unsupervised responsibility to persons with a propensity to engage in illegal activities.

(e) **Incentives for Compliance.** The organization has implemented a system of incentives, appropriate to its size and the nature of its business, to provide rewards (including, as appropriate, financial rewards) and recognition to employees and agents for their contributions to environmental excellence. In designing and implementing sales or production programs, the organization has insured that these programs are not inconsistent with the environmental compliance programs.

(f) **Disciplinary Procedures.** In response to infractions, the organization has consistently and visibly enforced the organization's environmental policies, standards and procedures through appropriate disciplinary mechanisms, including, as appropriate, termination, demotion, suspension, reassignment, retraining, probation, and reporting individuals' conduct to law enforcement authorities.

(g) **Continuing Evaluation and Improvement.** The organization has implemented a process for measuring the status and trends of its effort to achieve environmental excellence, and for making improvements or adjustments, as appropriate, in response to those measures and to any incidents of non-compliance. If appropriate to the size and nature of the organization, this should include a periodic, external evaluation of the organization's overall programmatic compliance effort, as reflected in these factors.

Commentary

Comment 1: The organization must carry the burden of demonstrating that it has made the substantial commitment necessary to be entitled to mitigation of the Base Fine. Under Step II(i) the demonstration should be made primarily by providing documentation, as of the time of the offense, pertaining to the factors described in this commentary.

Comment 2: For the definition of 'environmental requirements," see Comment 2 to Step II(i).

Comment 3: In assessing the extent of an organization's commitment, both the size and the nature of the organization are relevant. Ordinarily, organizations with larger numbers of operating facilities or pollution control activities and obligations should have more extensive and sophisticated environmental management systems, programs and resources of the nature described in this commentary than would be expected of similar, but smaller organizations. Similarly, organizations whose business activities may pose significant risks of harm to human health or the environment from noncompliance with environmental requirements (e.g. manufacture, use or management of hazardous products, materials or wastes) should have more extensive and sophisticated systems, programs and resources than would be expected of comparably sized organizations in less risky types of business.

Small organizations should demonstrate the same degree of commitment to environmental compliance as larger ones, although generally with less formality and less dedicated resources (if any) than would be expected of larger organizations. While each of the functions and objectives described in Step III should be substantially satisfied by all organizations, the small organization typically will rely on management personnel, operations personnel or others to assume compliance support responsibilities in addition to their routine duties, and will have less sophisticated systems for establishing compliance procedures, auditing and tracking compliance issues, training employees and carrying out the other programmatic components of their compliance effort. For example, in a very small business, the manager or proprietor, as opposed to independent compliance personnel, might perform routine audits with a simple checklist, train employees through informal staff meetings, and perform compliance monitoring through daily "walk-arounds" or continuous observation while managing the business. In appropriate circumstances, this reliance on existing resources and simple systems can demonstrate the same degree of commitment that, for a much larger organization, would require, for example, a full-time audit department, a training staff, an active compliance monitoring staff, and computer systems for tracking the resolution of compliance issues.

The essential requirement is that each organization must demonstrate, through appropriate documentation, that the resources and management processes it utilized were reasonably determined to be sufficient to perform the basic functions described in Step III. If, prior to the conviction, the organization had a reasonable basis to believe that its commitment of resources and processes would be sufficient, given its size and the nature of its business, then an appropriate mitigation value should be applied even though that commitment proved insufficient to prevent the offense of conviction.

Comment 4: In order to evaluate the demonstration of an organization's environmental compliance commitment, the documentation of its program or other organized effort, and the prosecution's challenges thereto, the court may engage such experts as it finds necessary, and the cost of such experts shall be paid by the organization. In its selection of such experts the court shall consider the recommendations of the prosecution and the defense. Any experts engaged by the court shall be given access to all information provided by the organization in support of its demonstration or its documentation, and to such other information as the court deems necessary for the expert to make an effective evaluation, taking into account any claims of privilege by the organization.

STEP IV:
GENERAL LIMITATIONS

(a)   **Limitation on Cumulative Effect of Mitigating Factors**

In no event may a fine determined under these guidelines be reduced as the result of mitigating factors to a level below the greater of (a) fifty percent [50%] of the Base Fine calculated in Step I or (b) the economic gain from the offense, if calculated under Step I(a)(1) in the determination of the Base Fine.

Commentary

Comment 1: To assure an adequate deterrent sufficient to deter third parties, the above provision specifies a floor below which the fine cannot be further reduced as the result of mitigating factors.

Example: Assume that in a given case the Base Fine was $1,000,000 and that the economic gain realized by the defendant corporation as a result of the crime was $600,000. On these facts, even if the mitigating factors recognized by the court to be present totalled $800,000, the fine could not be reduced below $600,000 (the "economic gain" from the offense). If there were no such cost savings, the fine could not be reduced below $500,000 (i.e., 50% of the Base Fine of $1,000,000).

Comment 2: This minimum floor provision does not limit the authority of the court to reduce the Base Fine by deleting the "unnecessary or repetitious counts" pursuant to Step I(b) of this sub-chapter or to depart from the guidelines in appropriate circumstances.

(b)   **Inability to Pay**

The court shall reduce the fine below that otherwise required to the extent that imposition of such fine would impair the defendant's ability to make restitution to the victim. The court may impose a fine below that otherwise required by this chapter if the court finds that:

(1) imposition of the required fine would result in the liquidation or cessation of all or a significant part of the business operations of the defendant due to the defendant's inability to pay the fine even with the use of a reasonable installment schedule;

(2) the defendant is not a "Criminal Purpose Organization" as described in § 8C1.1 of the Guidelines; and

(3) the defendant has not engaged in a sustained pattern of serious environmental violations.

The reduction allowed under Step IV(b) shall not be more than necessary to avert the threatened liquidation or cessation of business operations.

Questions for public comment:

1) Comment is solicited as to whether the limitation on the cumulative effect of mitigating factors should be framed in terms of a fixed reduction of the percentage of the Base Fine calculated in Step I rather than a fixed percentage of the Base Fine as the current draft envisages. For example, if the court determines that the appropriate percentage of maximum statutory fine, pursuant to Step I(a)(2)(a), for a knowing endangerment violation is 90%, and the limitation on the cumulative effect of mitigating factors is 50% pursuant to Step IV(a), the resulting limitation would be 40% of the Base Fine (90% - 50%). Similarly, if the court determines that the appropriate percentage of maximum statutory fine, pursuant to Step I(a)(2)(c), for an unlawful handling of a hazardous substance violation is 60%, and the limitation on mitigation pursuant to Step IV(a) is 50%, the resulting limitation would be 10% (60% - 50%).

2) Comment is solicited on whether 50% is the appropriate percentage under Step IV(a) for limitation on the cumulative effect of mitigating factors.

3) Comment is solicited on whether a limitation on the effect of aggravating factors should be included in Step IV(a) or a similar provision.

STEP V
PROBATION -- ORGANIZATIONS

(a)   **Imposition of Probation for Environmental Crimes - Organizations.**

The court shall order a term of probation if the court finds that:

(1) such sentence is advisable to secure payment of restitution (§ 8B1.1), enforce a remedial order (§ 8B1.2), or ensure completion of community service (§ 8B1.3); or

(2) the organization is sentenced to pay a monetary penalty (e.g., restitution, fine, or special assessment), the penalty is not paid in full at the time of sentencing, and restrictions are necessary to safeguard the organization's ability to make payments; or

(3) at the time of sentencing, the organization does not have an effective program to prevent and detect violations of law; or

(4) such sentence is advisable to ensure that changes are made within the organization to reduce the likelihood of future criminal conduct; or

(5) the organization within five years prior to sentencing engaged in similar misconduct, as determined by a prior criminal, civil, or administrative adjudication, and any part of the misconduct underlying the instant offense occurred after that adjudication; or

(6) any officer, manager, or supervisor within the organization or within the unit of the organization within which the instant offense was committed (a) participated in, (b) ordered, directed, or controlled the conduct of others in the commission of, or (c) consented to the misconduct underlying the instant offense and that individual within five years prior to sentencing engaged in similar misconduct, as determined by a prior criminal, civil, or administrative adjudication, and any part of the misconduct underlying the instant offense occurred after that adjudication; or

(7) the sentence imposed upon the organization does not include a fine; or

(8) such sentence is advisable to accomplish one or more of the purposes of sentencing set forth in 18 U.S.C. § 3553(a)(2).

(b)   **Term of Probation - Organizations**

(1) When a sentence of probation is imposed --

(i)   In the case of a felony, the term of probation shall be at least one year but not more than five years.

(ii)   In any other case, the term of probation shall be not more than five years.

Commentary

Application Note:

Within the limits set by the guidelines, the term of probation should be sufficient, but not more than necessary, to accomplish the court's specific objectives in imposing the term of probation.

(c)   **Conditions of Probation - Organizations**

(1) Pursuant to 18 U.S.C. § 3563(a)(1), any sentence of probation shall include the condition that the organization shall not commit another federal, state, or local crime during the term of probation.

(2) Pursuant to 18 U.S.C. § 3563(a)(2), if a sentence of probation is imposed for a felony, the court shall impose as a condition of probation at least one of the following: a fine, restitution, or community service, unless the court finds on the record that extraordinary circumstances exist that would make such condition plainly unreasonable, in which event the court shall impose one or more other conditions set forth in 18 U.S.C. § 3563(b).

(3) The court may impose other conditions that (1) are reasonably related to the nature and circumstances of the offense or the history and characteristics of the organization; and (2) involve only such deprivations of liberty or property as are necessary to effect the purposes of sentencing.

(4) If probation is ordered under Step V(a)(3) or (4), the court shall impose the conditions set forth in this paragraph. If probation is ordered under Step V(a)(5) or (6), the court shall impose any of the following conditions it deems necessary in order to achieve and maintain compliance with applicable environmental law. That determination of necessity shall be made in writing after the parties have had the opportunity to present relevant information to the court.

   (i)   The organization shall develop and submit to the Court a program to identify and correct any conditions that gave rise to the conviction and to prevent and detect any future violations, including (i) an effective program to detect and prevent future violations of law and (ii) a schedule of implementation of any such program.

   (ii)   Any such proposed program shall be made available for review by the government.

   (iii)   If the organization fails to submit a satisfactory program, the court shall engage such experts as it finds necessary to prepare such a program, and the cost of such experts shall be paid by the organization. Any experts engaged by the court shall be given access to such information in the possession of the organization as the court deems necessary to the effective accomplishment of the experts' task.

   (iv)   No program shall be approved that is less stringent than any applicable statutory or regulatory requirement.

   (v)   Upon approval by the court of a program to identify and correct any conditions that gave rise to the conviction and to prevent and detect violations of law, the organization shall notify its employees as the court deems appropriate and shall notify shareholders and the public of its criminal behavior and of the terms of the approved program. Such notice shall be in a form prescribed by the court.

(vi) The organization shall make periodic reports to the court, to the probation officer, or to any person or entity designated by the court, at intervals and in a form specified by the court, regarding the organization's progress in implementing the approved program. Among other things, such reports shall disclose any additional criminal prosecution, civil litigation involving its environmental responsibilities, or environmental administrative proceedings commenced against the organization, or any investigation or formal inquiry by governmental authorities relating to federal, state or local environmental health or safety matters of which the organization learned since it last report. Copies of any such periodic reports shall be furnished to the government.

(vii) In order to monitor the organization's compliance with the approved program, the court may order the organization to submit to such examination of its books and records, inspections of its facilities, testing and monitoring of its operation and regular or unannounced examinations of its employees as the court deems necessary. Compensation to and costs of any experts engaged by the court shall be paid by the organization. Reports on any such monitoring activities shall be filed with the court and copies shall be furnished to the government and the organization.

(5) If probation is imposed under Step V(a), the following conditions may be appropriate to the extent they appear necessary to safeguard the organization's ability to pay any deferred portion of an order of restitution, fine, or assessment.

(i) The organization shall make periodic submissions to the court or probation officer, at intervals specified by the court, reporting on the organization's financial condition and results of business operations, and accounting for the disposition of all funds received.

(ii) The organization shall submit to: (a) a reasonable number of regular or unannounced examinations of its financial or appropriate corporate books and records at appropriate business premises by the probation officer or experts engaged by the court; and (b) interrogation of knowledgeable individuals within the organization. Compensation to and costs of any experts engaged by the court shall be paid by the organization.

(iii) The organization shall be required to notify the court or probation officer immediately upon learning of (a) any material adverse change in its business or financial condition or prospects, or (b) the commencement of any bankruptcy proceeding, major civil litigation, criminal prosecution, or administrative proceeding against the organization, or any investigation or formal inquiry by governmental authorities regarding the organization.

(iv) The organization shall be required to make periodic payments, as specified by the court, in the following priority: (a) restitution; (2) fine; and (3) any other monetary sanction.

(d) **Additional Conditions of Probation (Policy Statement)**

The court may order the organization, at its expense and in the format and media specified by the court, to publicize the nature of the offense committed, the fact of conviction, the nature of the punishment imposed, and the steps that will be taken to prevent the recurrence of similar offenses.

Commentary

Application Notes:

1. In fashioning the conditions of probation, the court shall place particular emphasis on provisions requiring the organization to identify and correct the violations.

2. When probation is imposed under Step V(a)(5) or (6), it may not be necessary to include certain provisions of Step V(c). For example, certain provisions under Step V(c) would be unnecessary if the organization has a satisfactory compliance program in place, the offense is attributable to the actions of a particular employee, and that employee has been fired or severely disciplined.

3. In engaging any expert under Step V(c)(4)(iii) or (vii), the court shall submit to the organization and the government the identity and qualifications of any such expert who may be considered.

4. In order to assess the efficacy of a program submitted by the organization under Step V(c)(4)(i) or to permit an expert to prepare such a program under Step V(c)(4)(iii), the court shall order access to such material possessed by the organization as is necessary to a comprehensive evaluation of the proposed program.

5. In connection with the organization's submission of a report to the government regarding the existence and nature of any investigations or formal inquiries by governmental authorities, it may be appropriate for the organization to seek, and the court to grant, a protective order that preserves the confidentiality of such information.

(e) **Violations of Conditions of Probation - Organizations**
(Policy Statement)

Upon a finding of a violation of a condition of probation, the court may extend the term of probation, impose more restrictive conditions of probation, or revoke probation and resentence the organization.

Commentary

Application Note:

1. In the event of repeated, serious violations of conditions of probation, the appointment of a master or trustee may be appropriate to ensure compliance with court orders.

   ### Questions for public comment:

   1) Comment is solicited on whether organizations should be required to notify shareholders of any environmental conviction.

   2) Comment is solicited on whether organizations should be required to notify employees at a facility when the organization is convicted of environmental crimes at that facility.

SUBJECT INDEX

Audits, See Environmental Audits

CERCLA, Reporting Violations under   38
Chemicals, Regulation of   39
Clean Air Act   27
    Emission Restrictions under   28
    Failure to Pay Fees under   29
    False Statements under   28
    Increased Corporate Prosecutions under   31
    Knowing Endangerment under   30
    Negligent Endangerment under   29
Clean Water Act
    Criminal Provisions of Original Act   32
    Water Quality Act of 1987 Amendments 33
Collective Knowledge Doctrine   25
Compliance Diagnostic   51
    Collection and Review of Background Materials   54
    Contracts with Waste Haulers and Disposal Facilities   56
    Initial Focus of   53
    Protecting Confidentiality of   56
    Purpose and Objectives of   52
    Review of Agency Records   55
    Scope of   54
    Site Assessments   55
Consultants and Contractors
    Contracts with   59
    Role of   58
    Specific Contract Issues   61
        Approval of Subcontractors   63
        Condition of the Site   66
        Disposal of Wastes   67
        Exclusive Use Provision   62
        Indemnification   63
        Independent Contractor Status   62
        Insurance   67
        Key Personnel   68
        Laboratories   68
        Limitations of Liability   65
        Major Changes and Delays   65
        Retention and Confidentiality of Records   69
        Standard of Care   61
        Warranty of Non-Disbarment   70

Criminal Fines Improvements Act of 1987   44
Criminal Investigations
      Government Use of Search Warrants   83
      Limits on Search Warrants   84
      Receipt of the Warrant/Monitoring the Investigation 85
      Responding Appropriately to   83
Criminal Prosecution
      of Corporations   3, 77
            under Clean Air Act   31
      of Individuals   79
      Justice Dept. Guidance on, See Factors in Decisions
      Reducing the Likelihood of Being a Target of   80
      Selection of Targets for   71
Criminal Statutes, General   42

Enforcement
      Federal   1
      Joint Federal-State   10
      State and Local Prosecution   6
Environmental Audits (See also Compliance Diagnostic)   46
      Costs and Risks of   51
      Government Encouragement of   46
      Protecting Confidentiality of   56
      Voluntary Audit/Compliance Guidelines   114
Environmental Crimes in Federal Statutes   42
EPCRA, Reporting Violations under   38

Factors in Decisions on Criminal Prosecutions   72, 122
      Cooperation   74
      Internal Disciplinary Action   76
      Pervasiveness of Noncompliance   76
      Preventive Measures and Compliance Programs   74
      Subsequent Compliance Efforts   77
      Voluntary Disclosure   73
Federal Enforcement   1
Federal Environmental Statutes   26
Federal Insecticide Fungicide and Rodenticide Act   39
Federal Sentencing Guidelines   91, 132
      Fines under   95
      for Individuals   91
      for Organizations   94
      Probation and Other Non-Monetary Penalties under   97

Government Encouragement of Audits   46
Government Use of Search Warrants   83

Investigations, <u>See</u> Criminal Investigations

Joint Federal-State Enforcement   10
Justice Department
    Guidance on Criminal Prosecution, <u>See</u> Factors in Decisions
    Procedures, U.S. Attorneys' Offices & Headquarters   101

Knowing Endangerment
    under Clean Air Act   30
    under Clean Water Act   33
    under Resource Conservation and Recovery Act   37

Occupational Safety and Health Act   41
Outside Contractors, <u>See</u> Consultants and Contractors

Prosecutorial Discretion
    Criminal Actions Against Companies   77
    Criminal Actions Against Individuals   79
    Justice Dept. Guidance, <u>See</u> Factors in Decisions
    Selection of Targets for Criminal Prosecution   71

Reducing the Likelihood of Being an Enforcement Target   80
Regulation of Chemicals, <u>See</u> Chemicals
Regulatory Crimes   11
Reporting Violations under CERCLA and EPCRA   38
Resource Conservation and Recovery Act   36
    Criminal Provisions   36
    Knowing Endangerment under   37
Responding Appropriately to Criminal Investigations   83
Responsible Corporate Officer Doctrine   17
    in Federal Statutes   21
    in State Statutes   23

Search Warrants
    Government Use of   83
    Limits on   84
    Receipt of   85
Sentencing, <u>See</u> Federal Sentencing Guidelines
State and Local Prosecution   6

Toxic Substances Control Act   40

U.S. Attorneys' Offices, <u>See</u> Justice Department, Procedures
U.S. Department of Justice, <u>See</u> Justice Department

Voluntary Environmental Audit/Compliance Guidelines   114

About Government Institutes

Government Institutes, Inc. was founded in 1973 to provide continuing education and practical information for your professional development. Specializing in environmental, health and safety concerns, we recognize that you face unique challenges presented by the ever-increasing number of new laws and regulations and the rapid evolution of new technologies, methods and markets.

Our information and continuing education efforts include a Videotape Distribution Service, over 140 courses held nation-wide throughout the year, and over 150 publications, making us the world's largest publisher in these areas.

Government Institutes, Inc.
4 Research Place, Suite 200
Rockville, MD 20850
(301) 921-2300

Other related books published by Government Institutes:

Environmental Law Handbook, 12th Edition - The recognized authority in the field, this invaluable text, written by nationally-recognized legal experts, provides practical and current information on all major environmental areas. Hardcover/670 pages/Apr '93/$68 ISBN: 0-86587-350-X

Environmental Statutes, 1993 Edition - All the major environmental laws incorporated into one convenient source.
Hardcover/1,170 pages/Mar '93/$59   ISBN: 0-86587-352-6
Softcover/1,170 pages/Mar '93/$49   ISBN: 0-86587-351-8

Environmental Regulatory Glossary, 6th Edition - This glossary records and standardizes more than 4,000 terms, abbreviations and acronyms, all compiled directly from the environmental statutes or the U.S. Code of Federal Regulations. Hardcover/544 pages/May '93 $65   ISBN: 0-86587-353-4

Directory of Environmental Information Sources, 4th Edition - Details hard-to-find Federal Government Resources; State Government Resources; Professional, Scientific, and Trade Organizations; Newsletters, Magazines, and Periodicals; and Databases.
Softcover/350 pages/Nov '92/$74   ISBN: 0-86587-326-7

Environmental Audits, 6th Edition - Details how to begin and manage a successful audit program for your facility. Use these checklists and sample procedures to identify your problem areas. Softcover/ 592 pages/Nov '89/$75   ISBN: 0-86587-776-9

The Greening of American Business: Making Bottom-Line Sense of Environmental Responsibility - Written by leading environmental professionals from industry, law firms, and universities, this book explains how companies are coping with increasing demands that they engage in environmentally-sound business practices. Softcover 350 pages/Oct '92/$24.95   ISBN: 0-86587-295-3

Call the above number for our current book/video catalog and course schedule.

Environmental Insurance Handbook - This handbook provides clear, concise explanations of the environmental insurance coverage issues. Chapters include: Overview of the Environmental Laws, Coverage Under CGL Policies, Locating and Maintaining Policies, Notifying Insurers of Environmental Claims, Scope and Trigger of Environmental Claims, Policy Exclusions, and Strategies for Coverage Litigation. Softcover/490 pages/Oct '92/$74 ISBN: 0-86587-325-9

Superfund Manual: Legal and Management Strategies, 5th Edition - This manual clearly explains hazardous substance release reporting, liability and enforcement, the national contingency plan and the NPL, response strategies, uses of the superfund, EPCRA, and much more. Includes a copy of the Superfund Amendments and Reauthorization Act of 1986. Softcover/468 pages/May '93/$95 ISBN: 0-86587-344-5

RCRA Hazardous Wastes Handbook, 10th Edition - The Washington, D.C. law firm of Crowell & Moring gives you clear, concise answers to take you step-by-step through the maze of RCRA/Hazardous Wastes regulations. Includes the RCRA Statute. Softcover/464 pages/ Oct '93/$110 ISBN: 0-86587-355-0

Clean Water Handbook - Written by attorneys J. Gorden Arbuckle and Russell V. Randle of the Washington, D.C. law firm of Patton, Boggs & Blow, along with a team of other legal and technical experts, this comprehensive handbook offers a straightfoward explanation of how the clean water laws and regulations affect your business. Softcover/446 pages/June '90/$85 ISBN: 0-86587-210-4

Clean Air Handbook - Provides a clear explanation of the Clean Air Act including the 1990 Amendments and how they will affect businesses. This handbook covers: regulatory issues and the nonattainment puzzle; NAAQ standards; emerging air quality issues; source performance standards; air toxics regulations; permits and pre-construction review; and stationary and mobile source regulations. Softcover/336 pages/Mar '91/$79 ISBN: 0-86587-239-2

Educational Programs

■ Our **COURSES** combine the legal, regulatory, technical, and management aspects of today's key environmental, safety and health issues — such as environmental laws and regulations, environmental management, pollution prevention, OSHA and many other topics. We bring together the leading authorities from industry, business and government to shed light on the problems and challenges you face each day. Please call our Education Department at (301) 921-2345 for more information!

■ Our **TRAINING CONSULTING GROUP** can help audit your ES&H training, develop an ES&H training plan, and customize on-site training courses. Our proven and successful ES&H training courses are customized to fit your organizational and industry needs. Your employees learn key environmental concepts and strategies at a convenient location for 30% of the cost to send them to non-customized, off-site courses. Please call our Training Consulting Group at (301) 921-2366 for more information!

Government Institutes, Inc., 4 Research Place, Suite 200, Rockville, MD 20850, (301) 921-2300